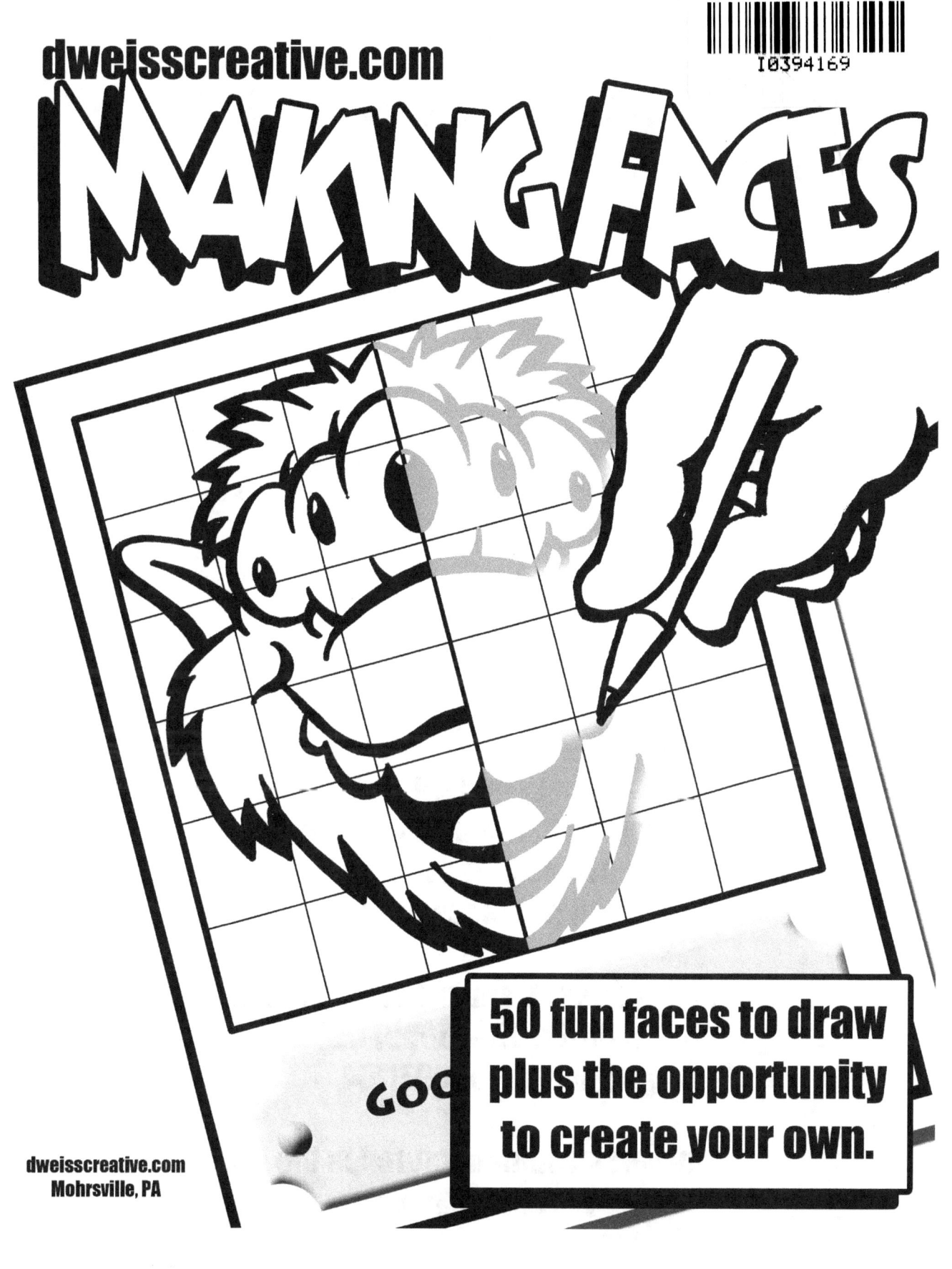

International Standard Book Number
ISBN-13: 978-1505971767
ISBN-10: 1505971764

Print version manufactured in the U.S.
by CreateSpace.com

SO HOW DOES THIS WORK?

Let's start by drawing this handsome fellow...

1. Start in the center and duplicate what you see in the opposite square only backwards.

2. Work your way down the page and across the grid until the drawing is complete, copying as closely as you can.

3. When you finish, add color and decorate your picture.

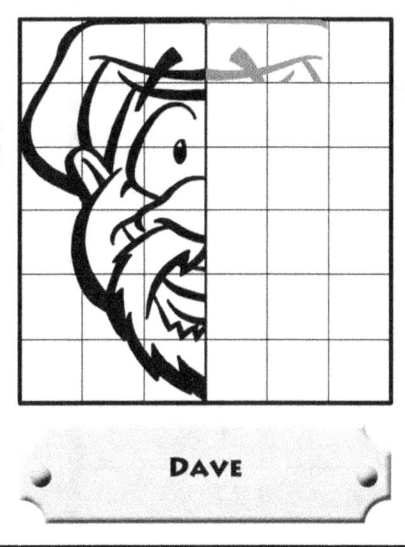

DAVE

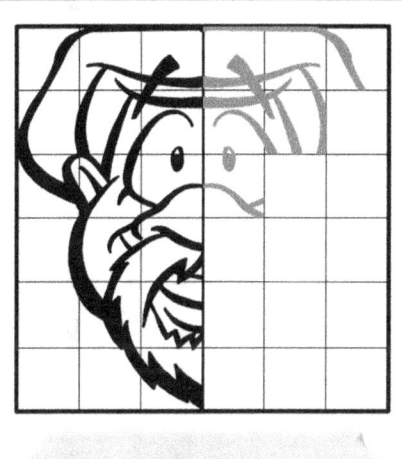

DAVE

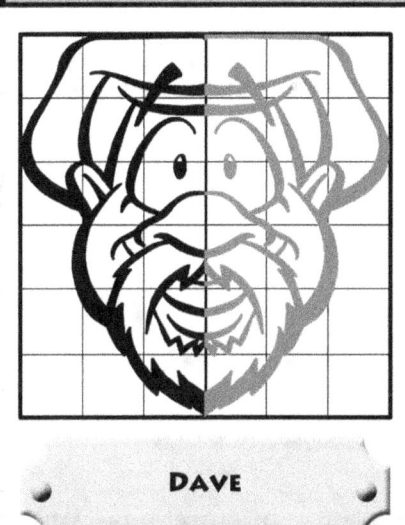

DAVE

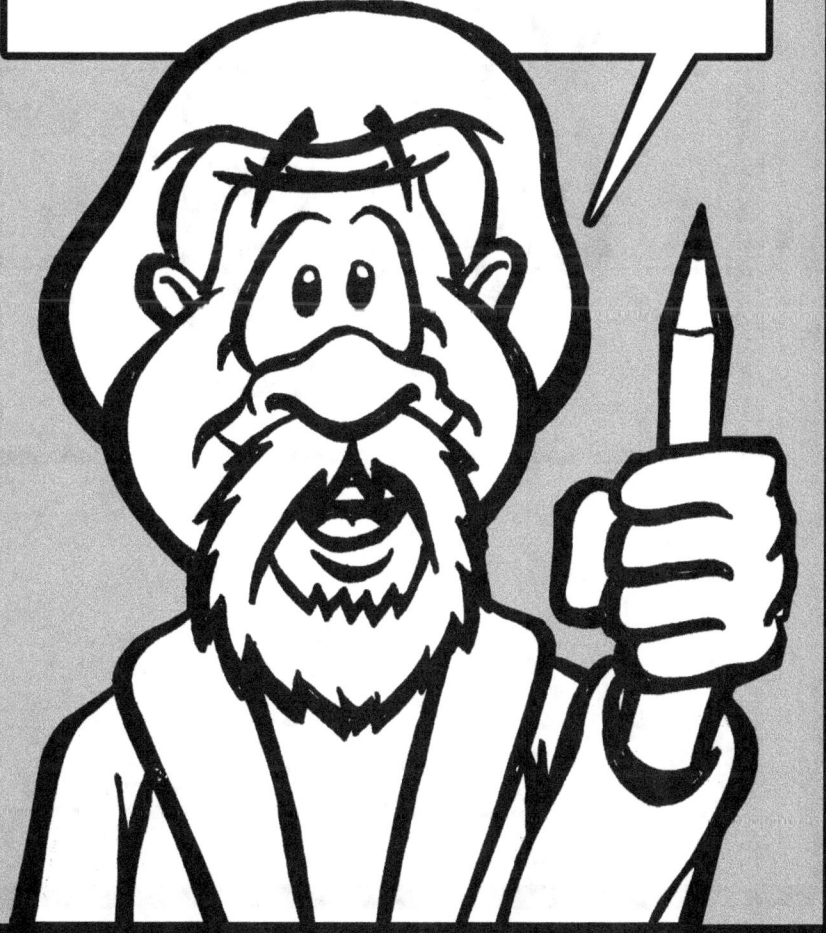

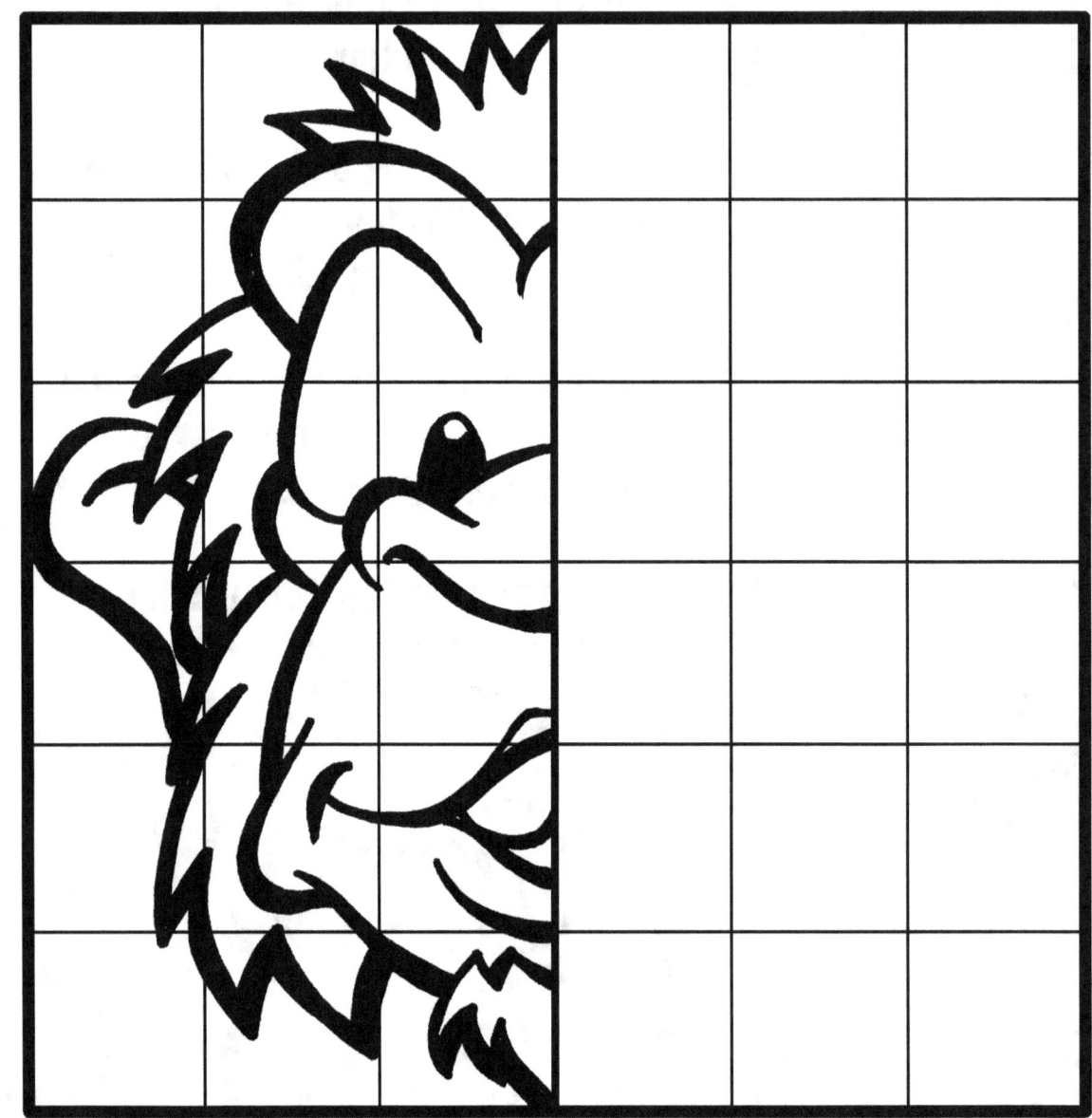

BONZO

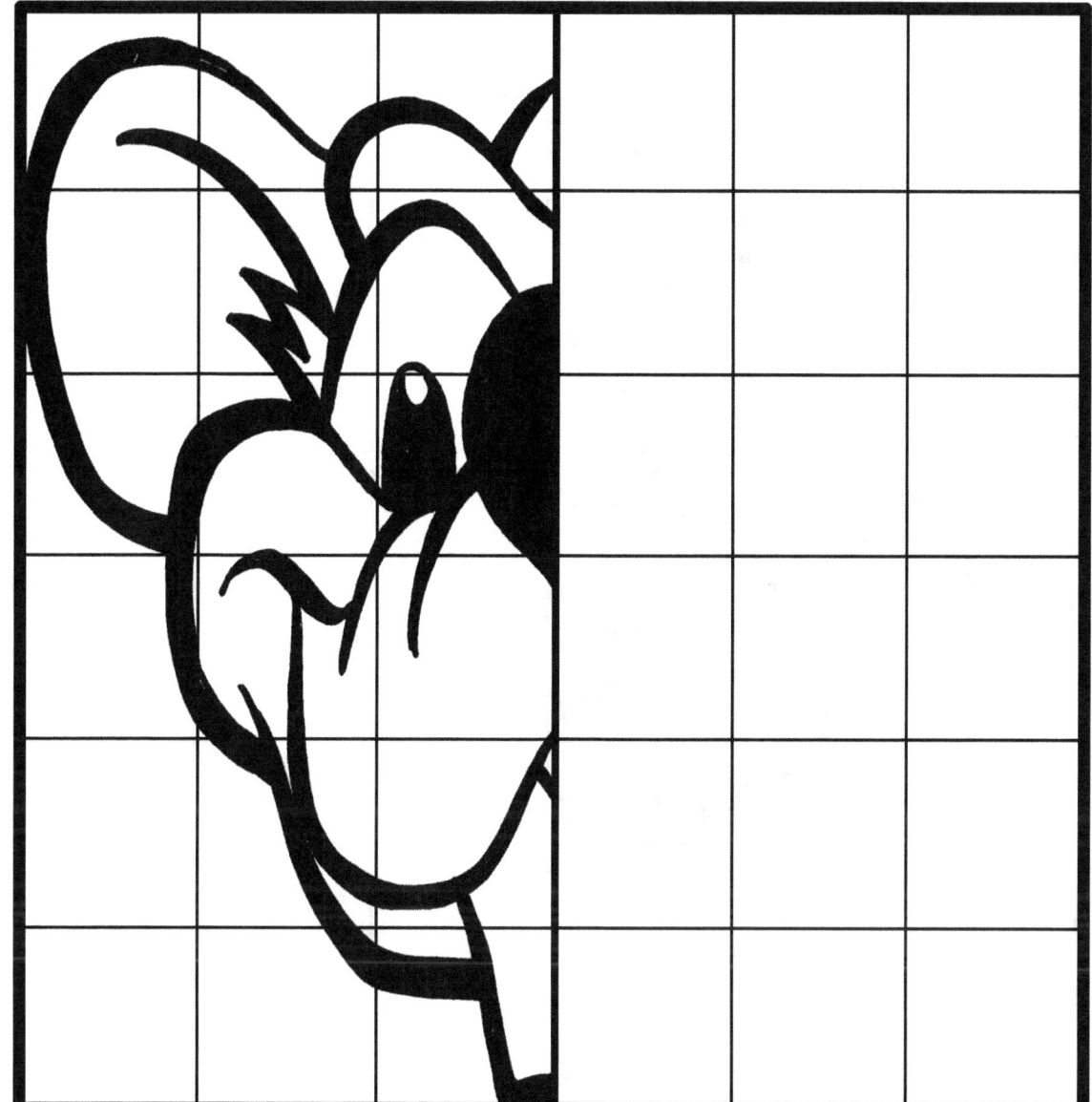

RATICAL

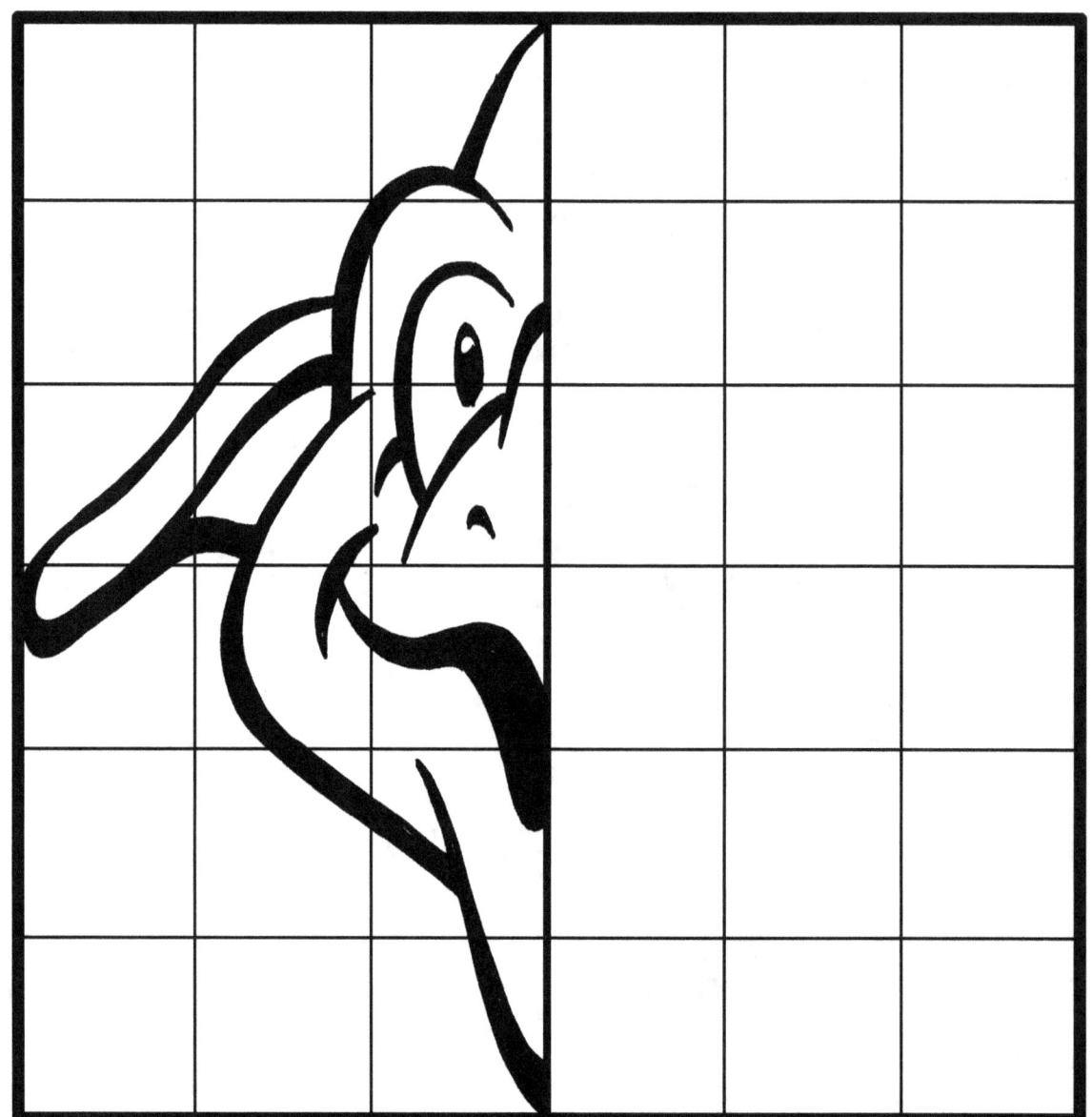

BINGO

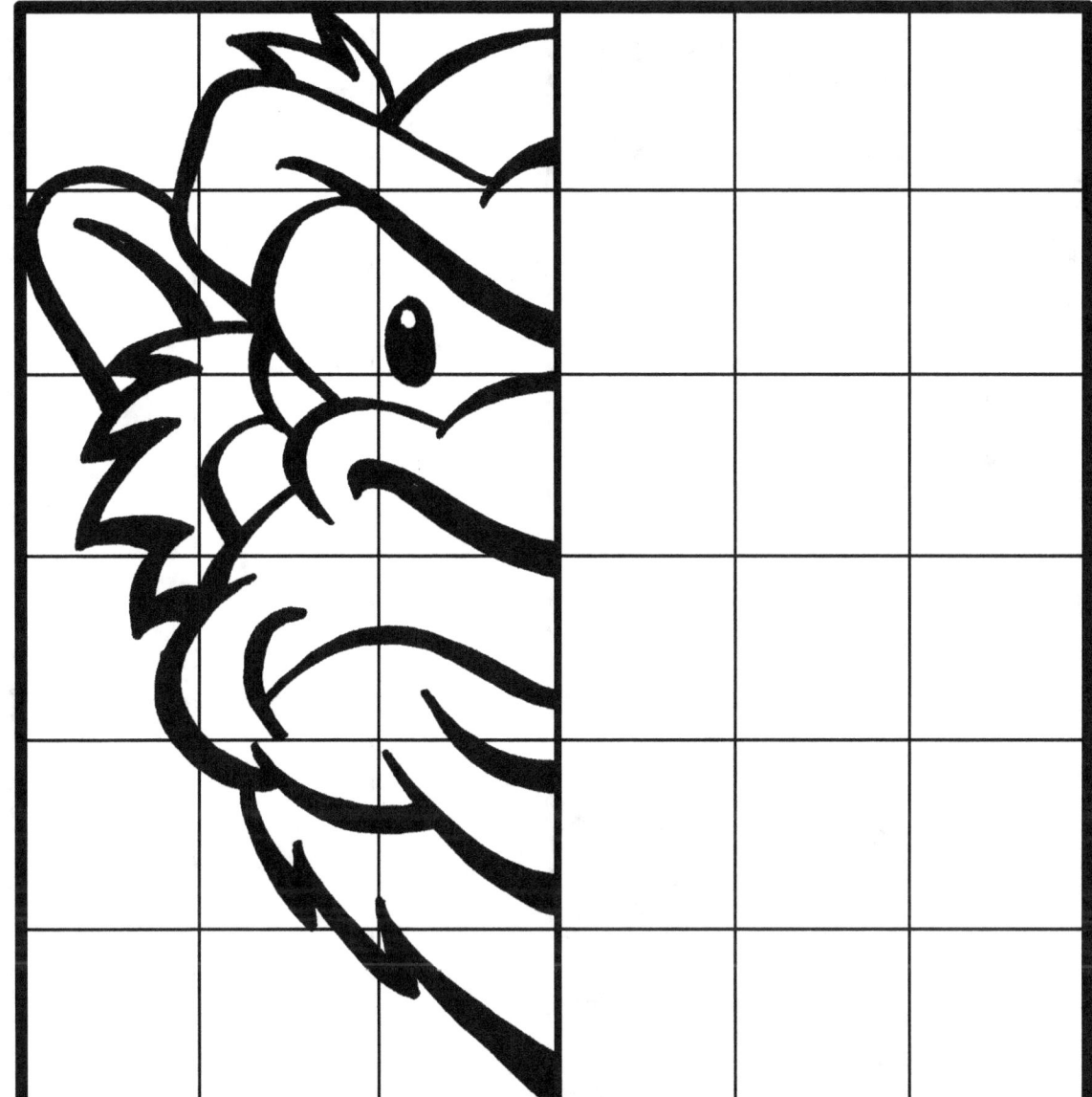

GRUMP

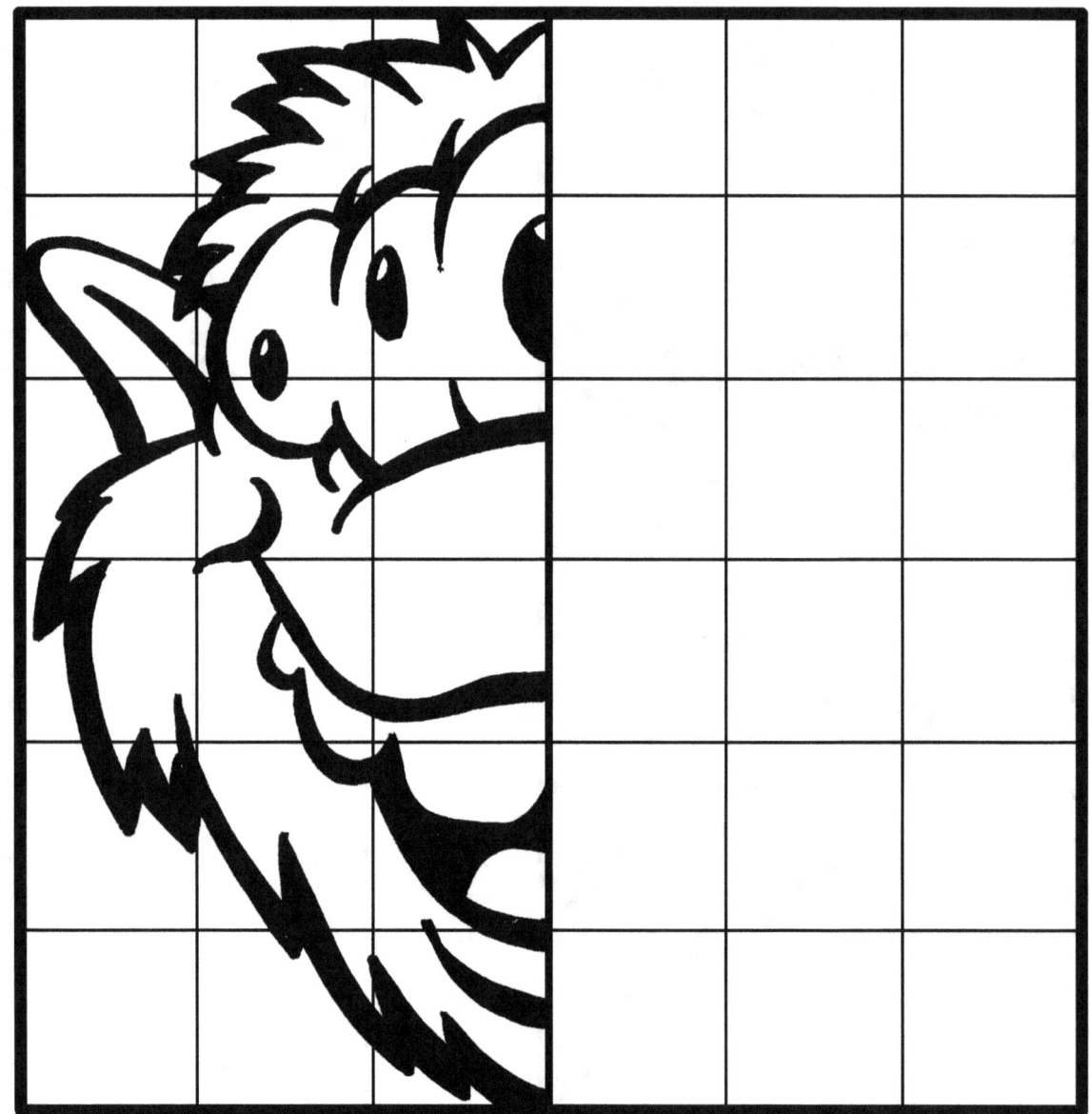

GOOGLY MOOGLY

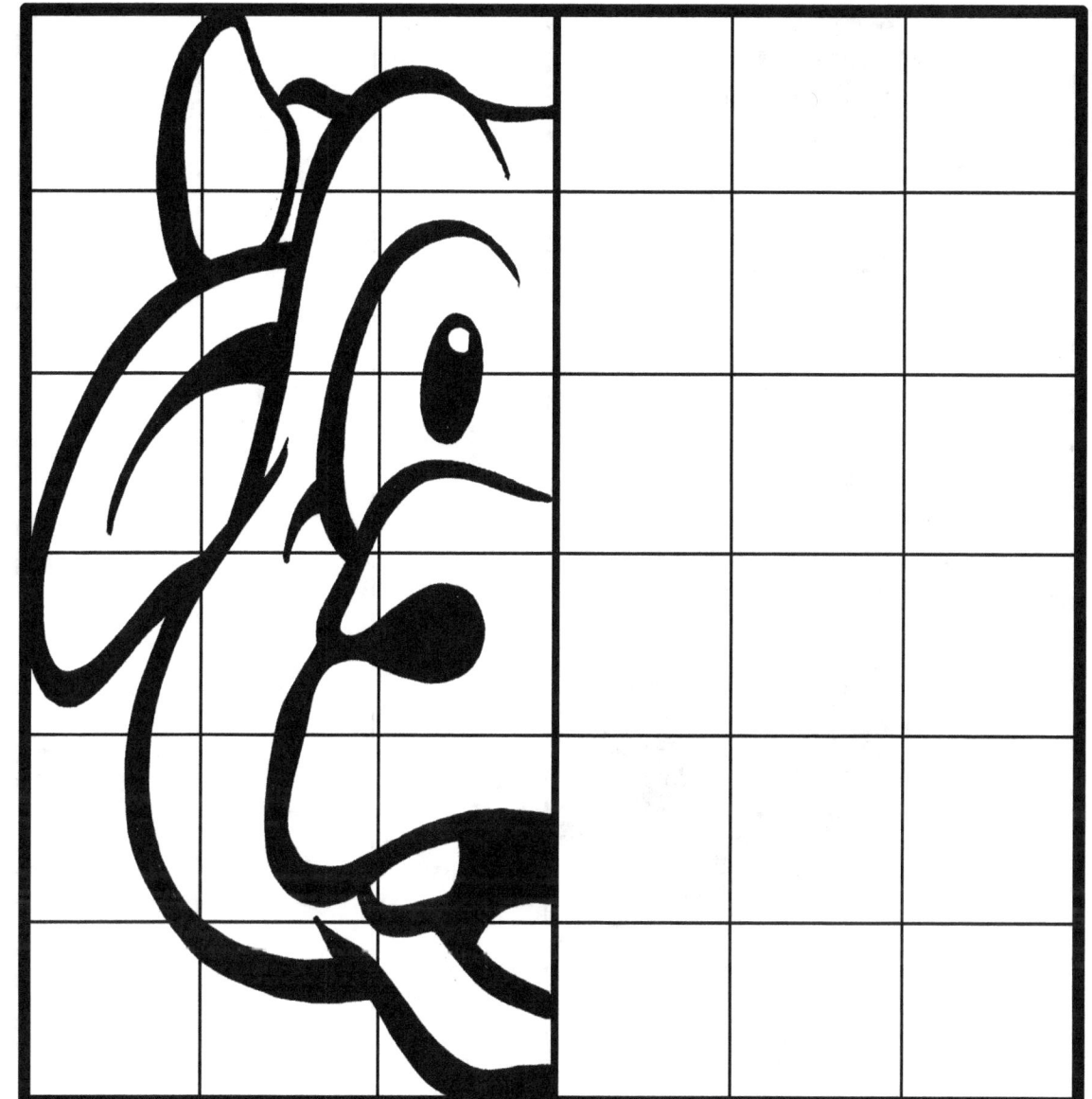

MOONERD

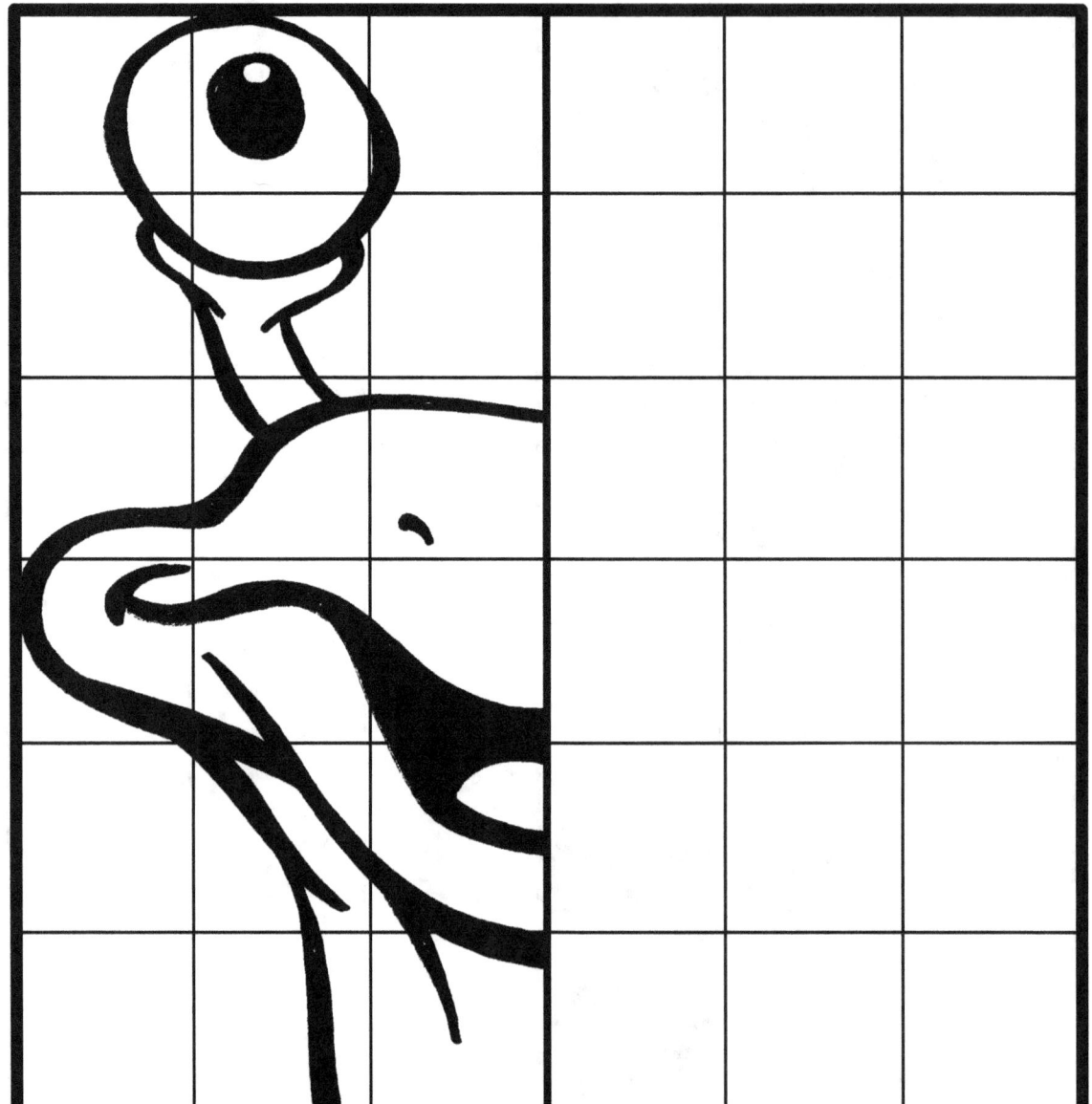

S-CAR-GO!

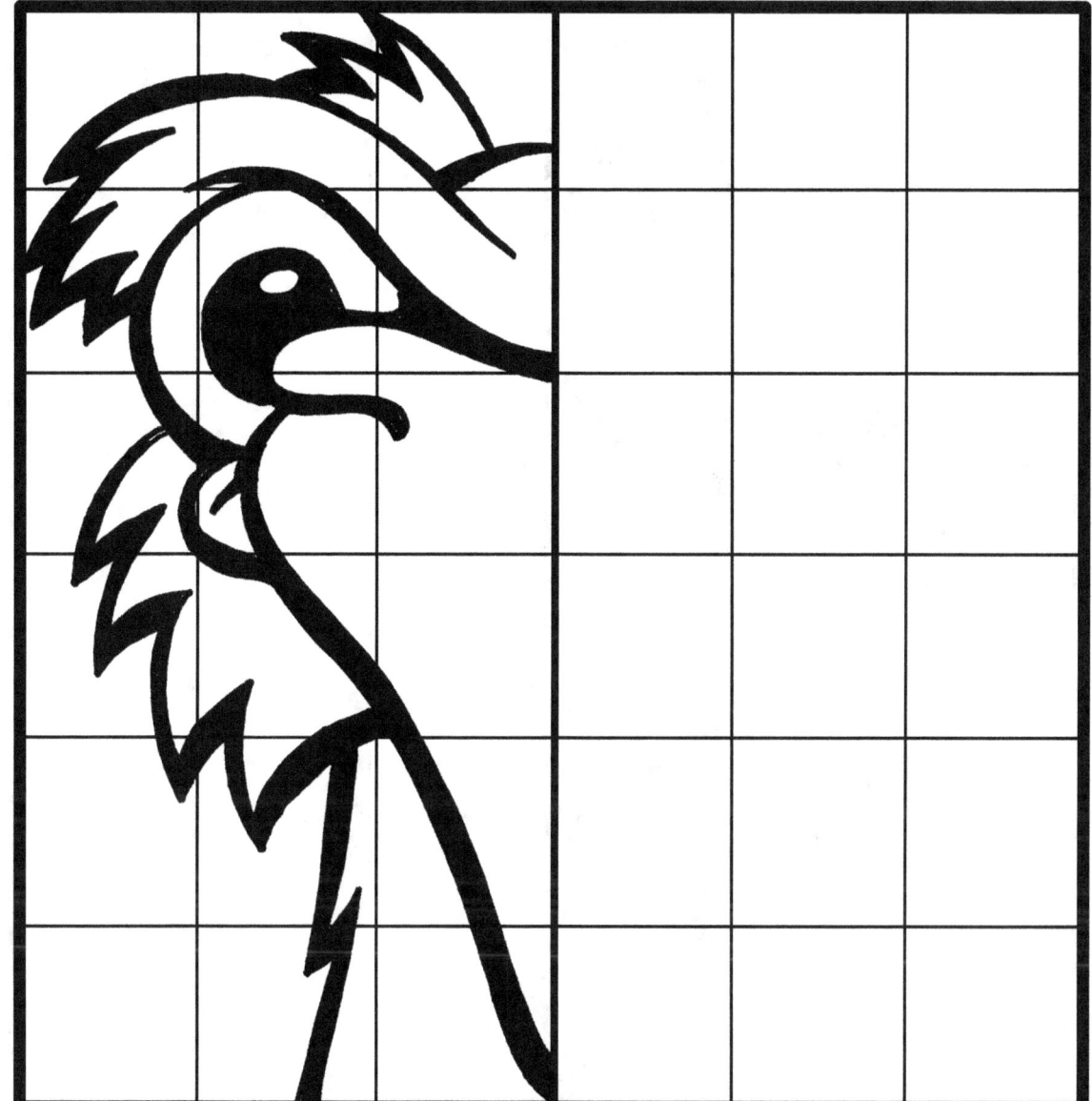

EMOEMU

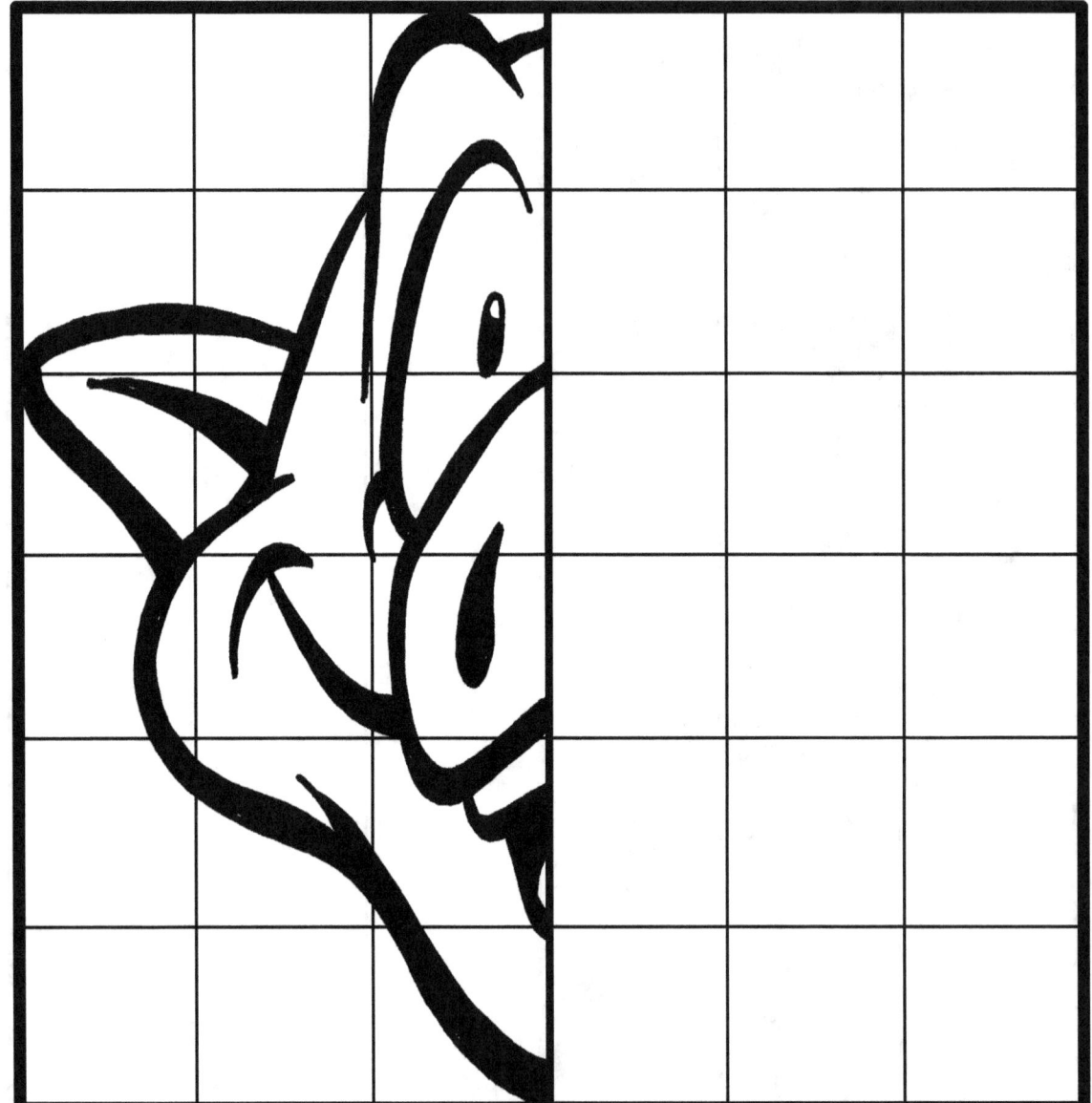

SQUOINKER

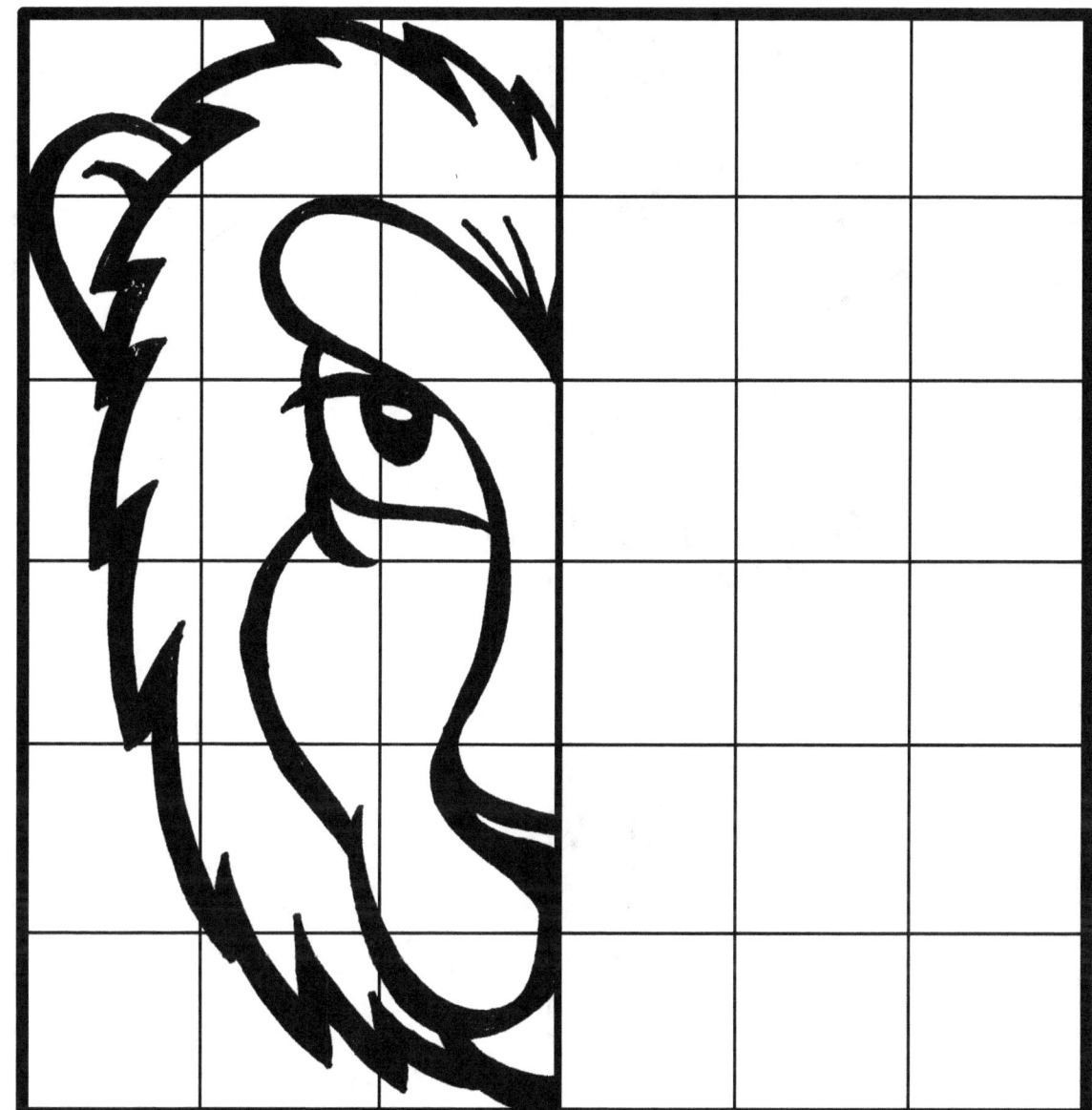

MIDAS

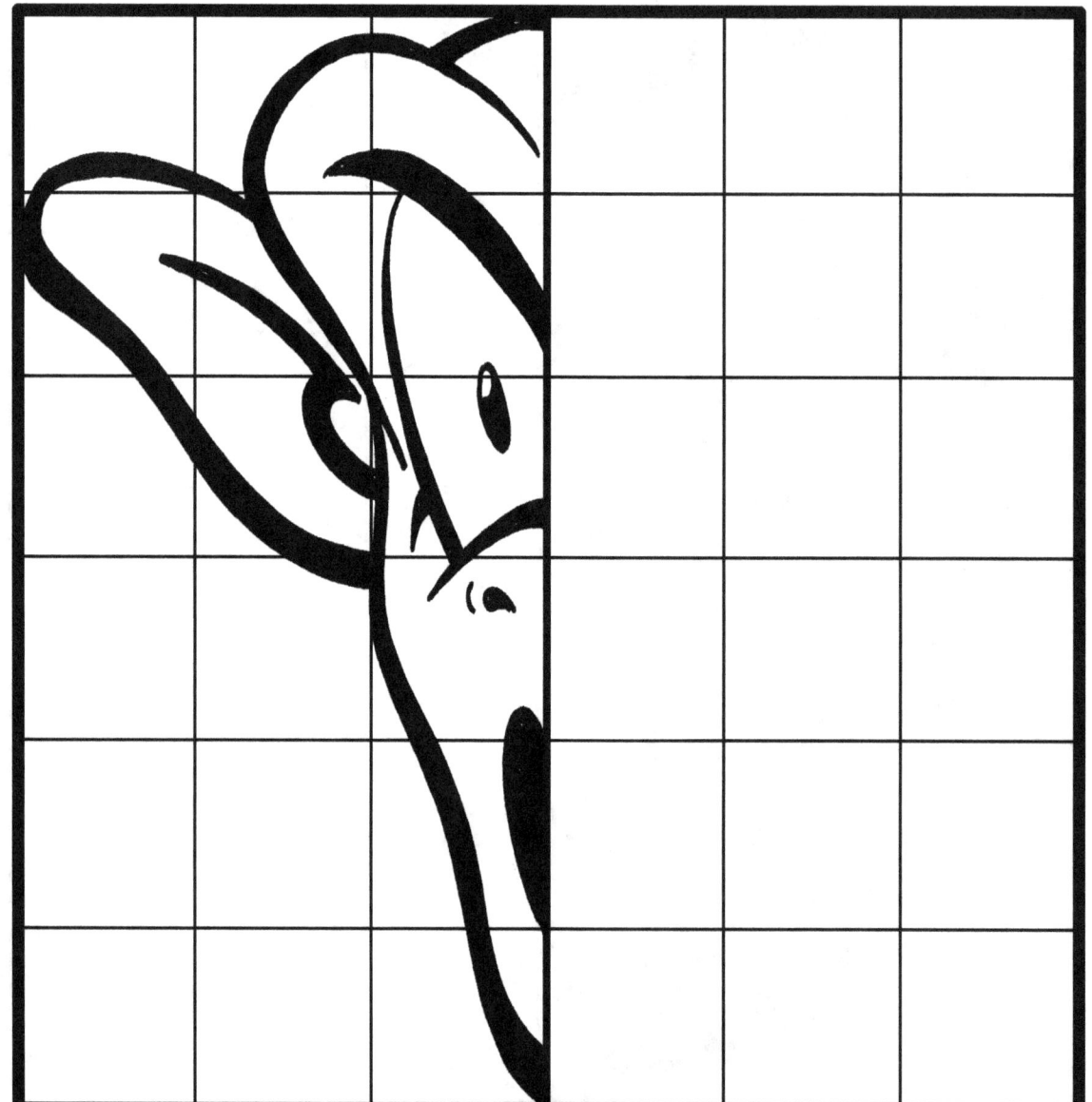

RAGE-O

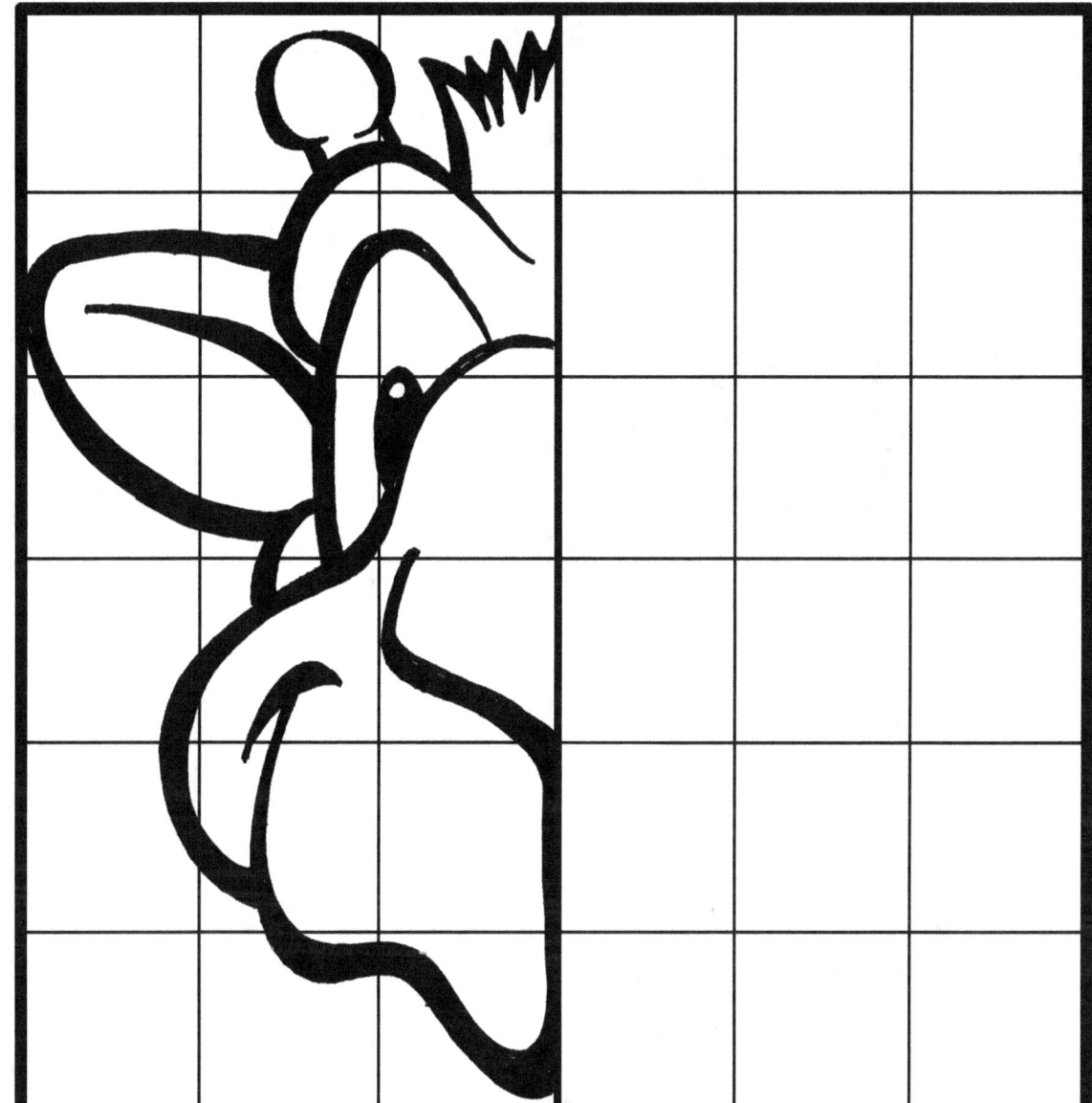

STRETCH

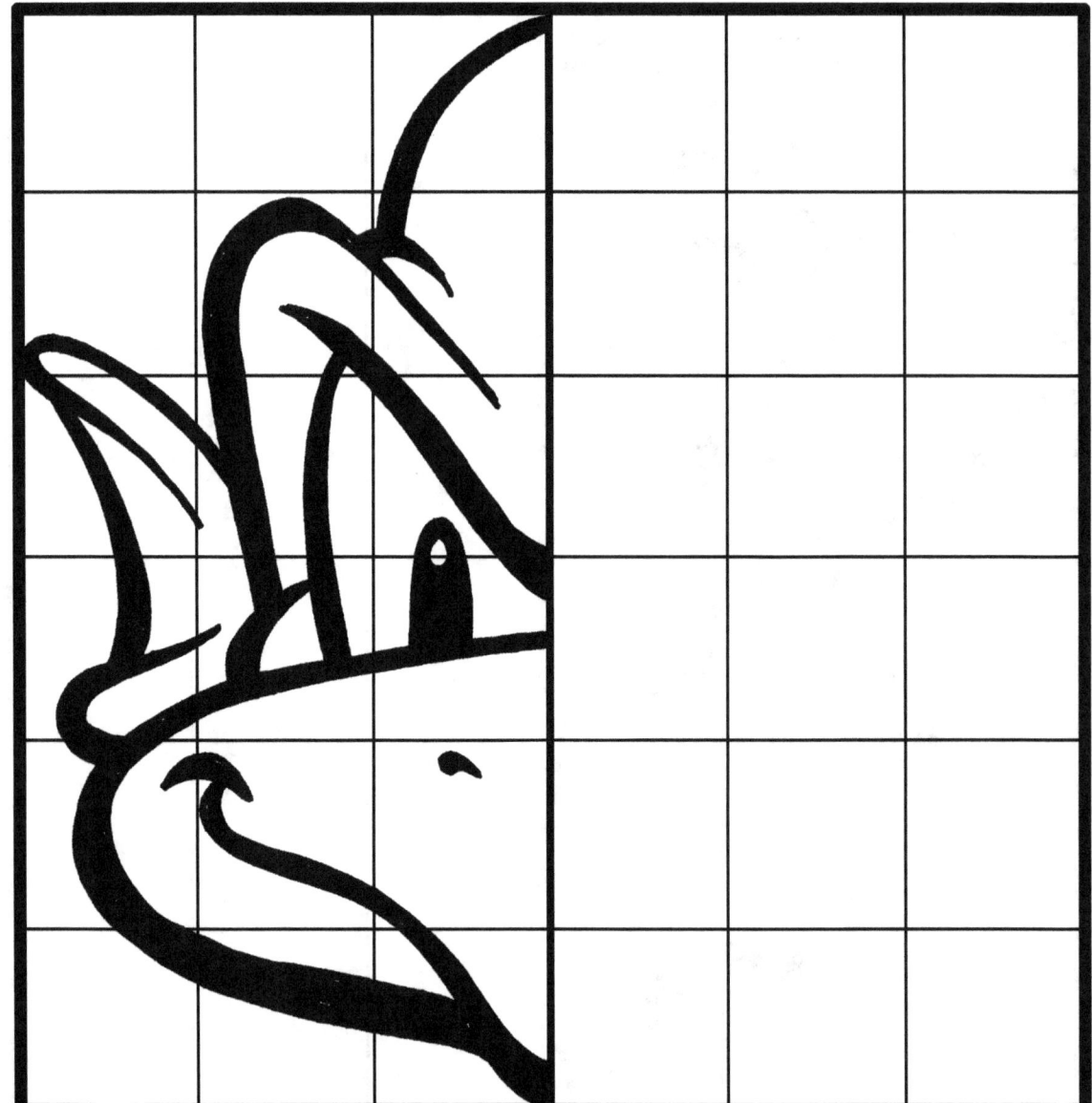

BLARGH

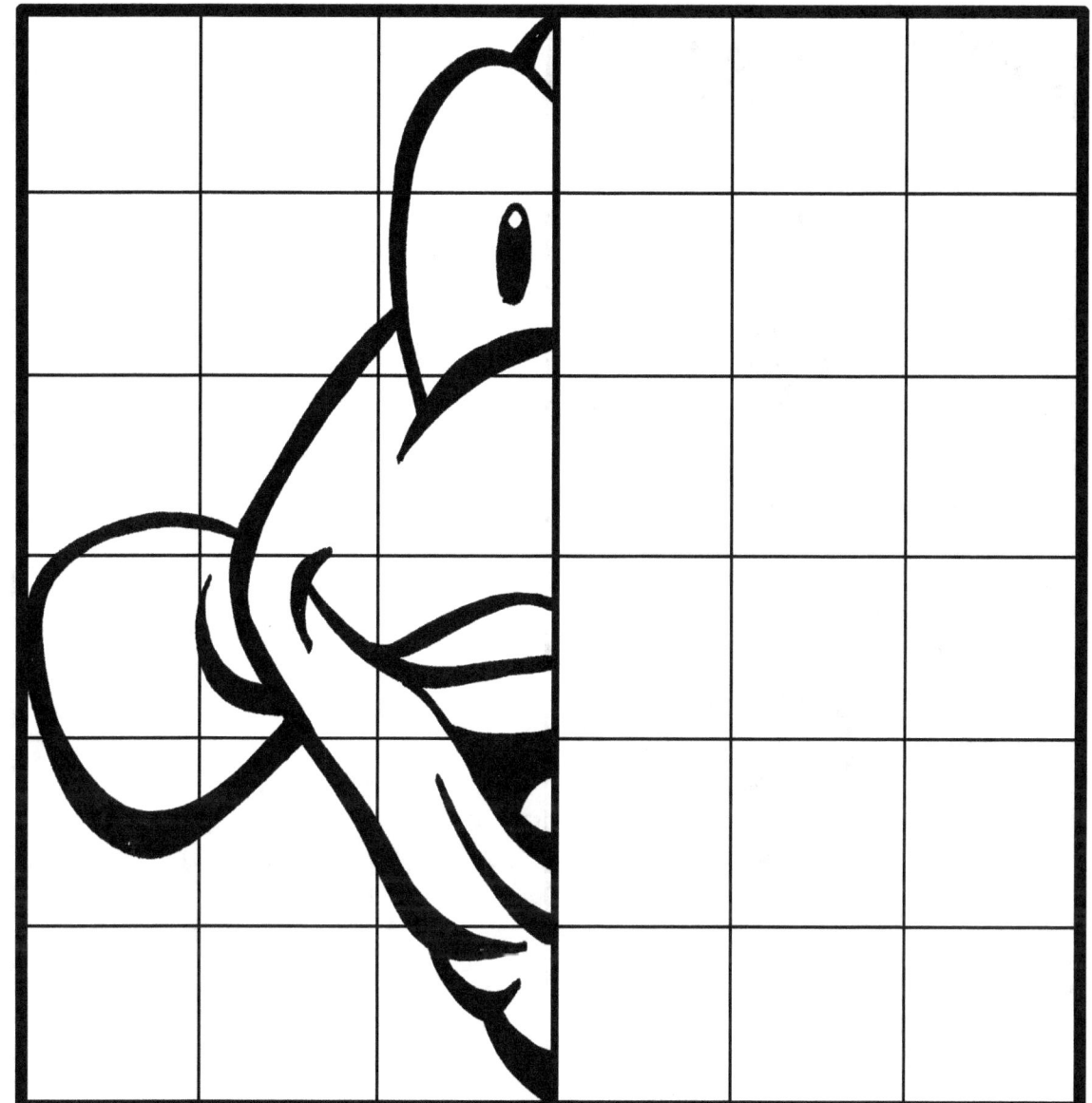

FISHYDEMUS

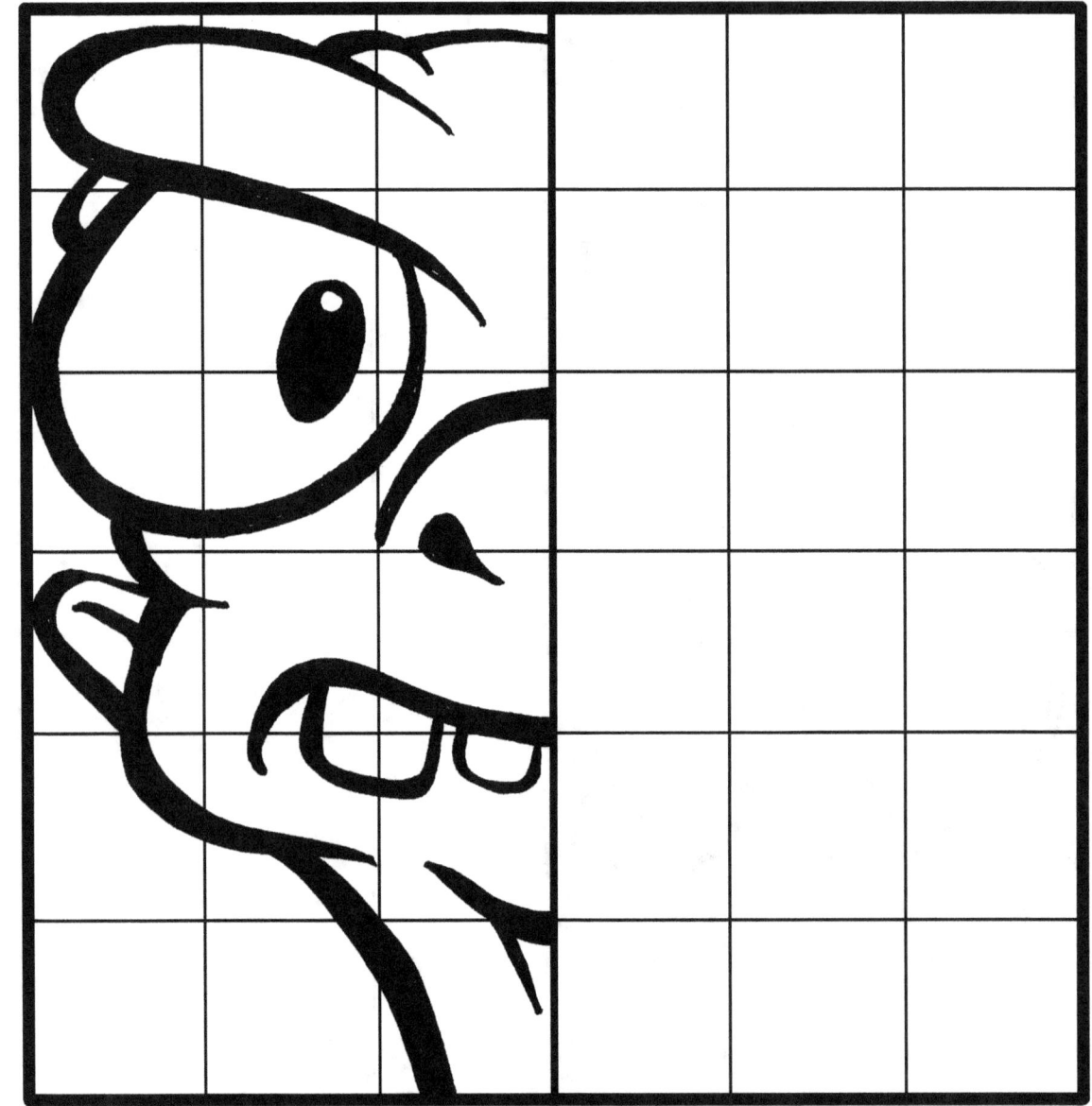

DOOFENHEIMER

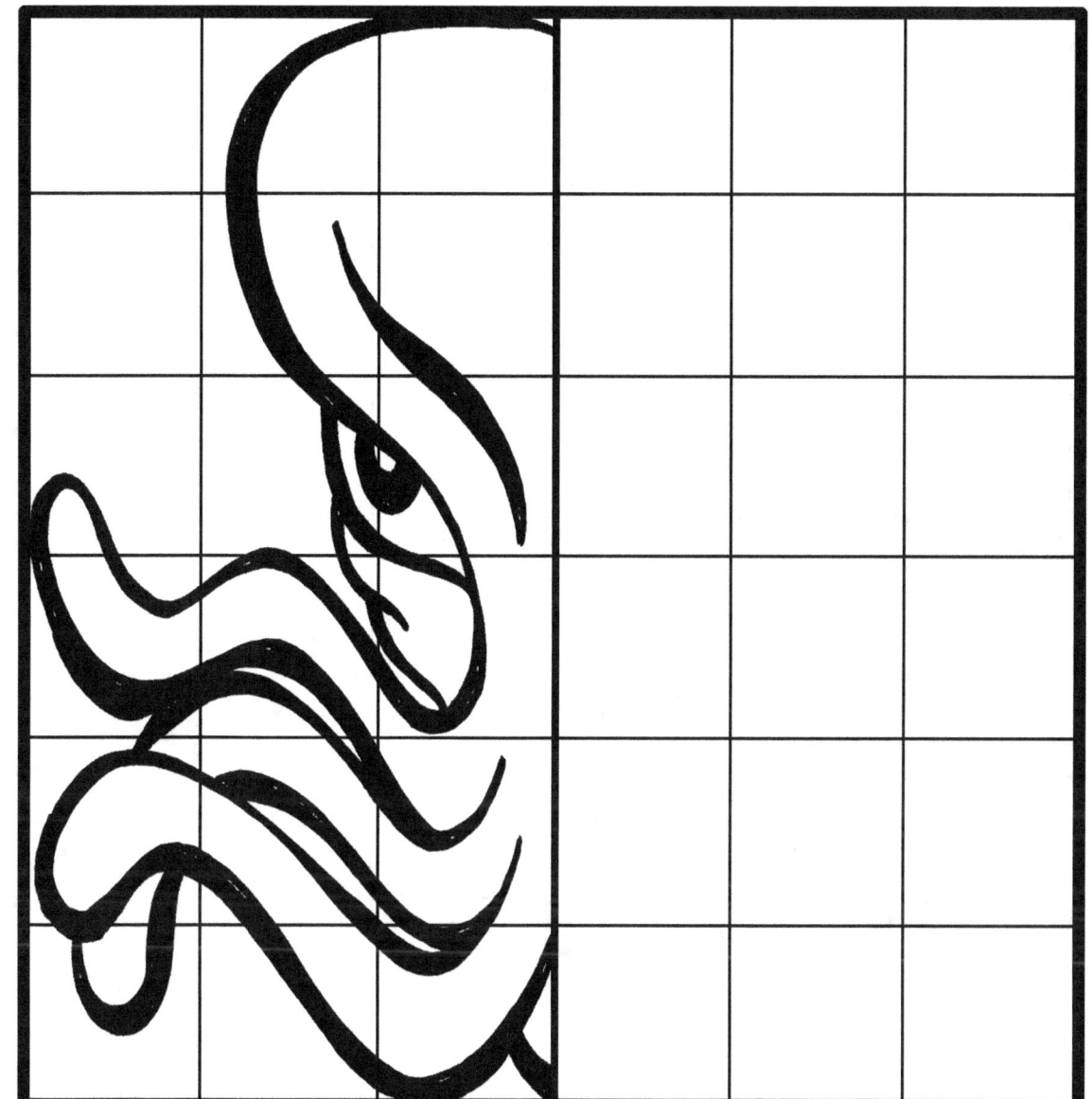

CRACKEN

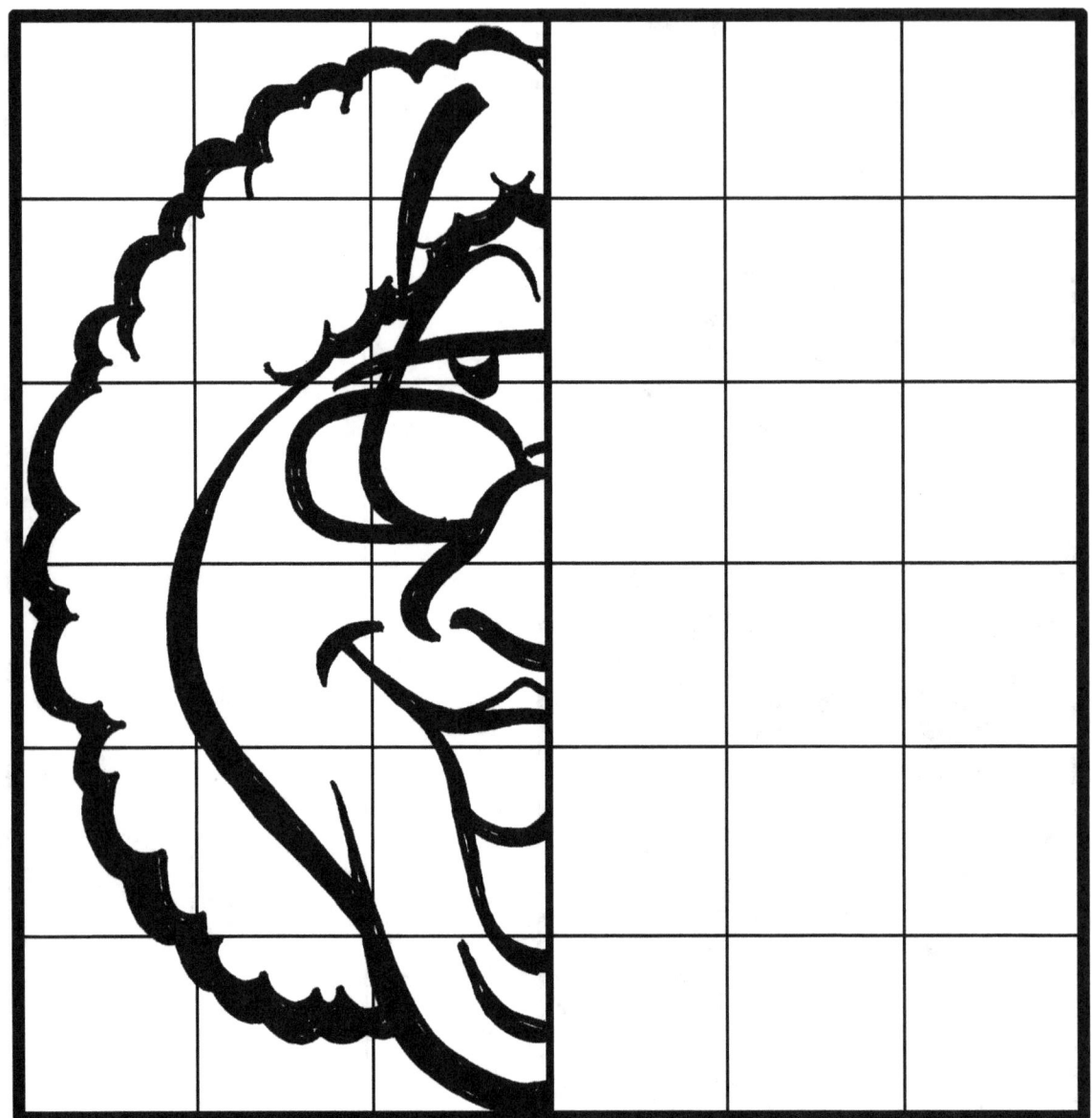

MISS FRUMP

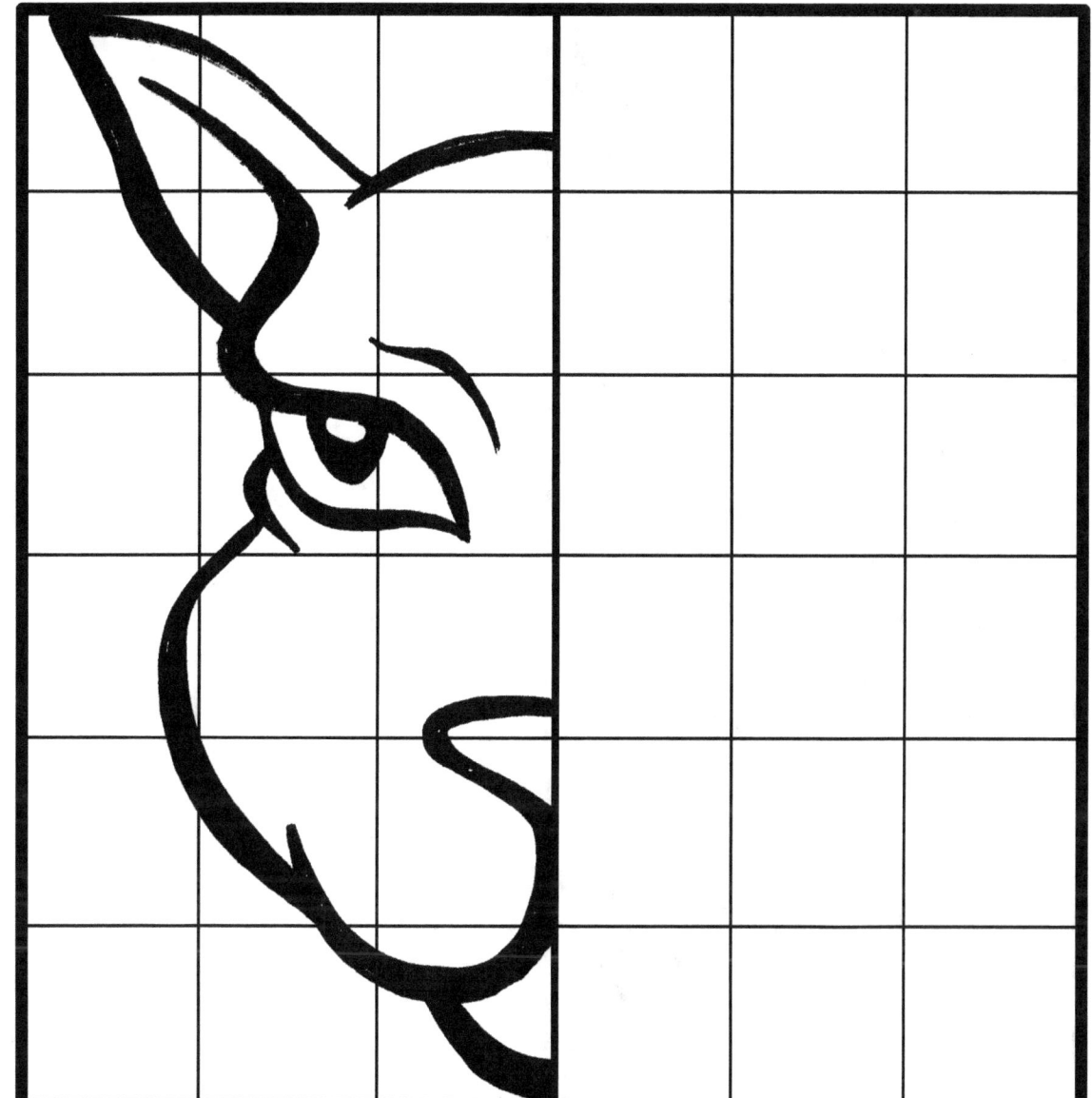

PRETTY KITTY

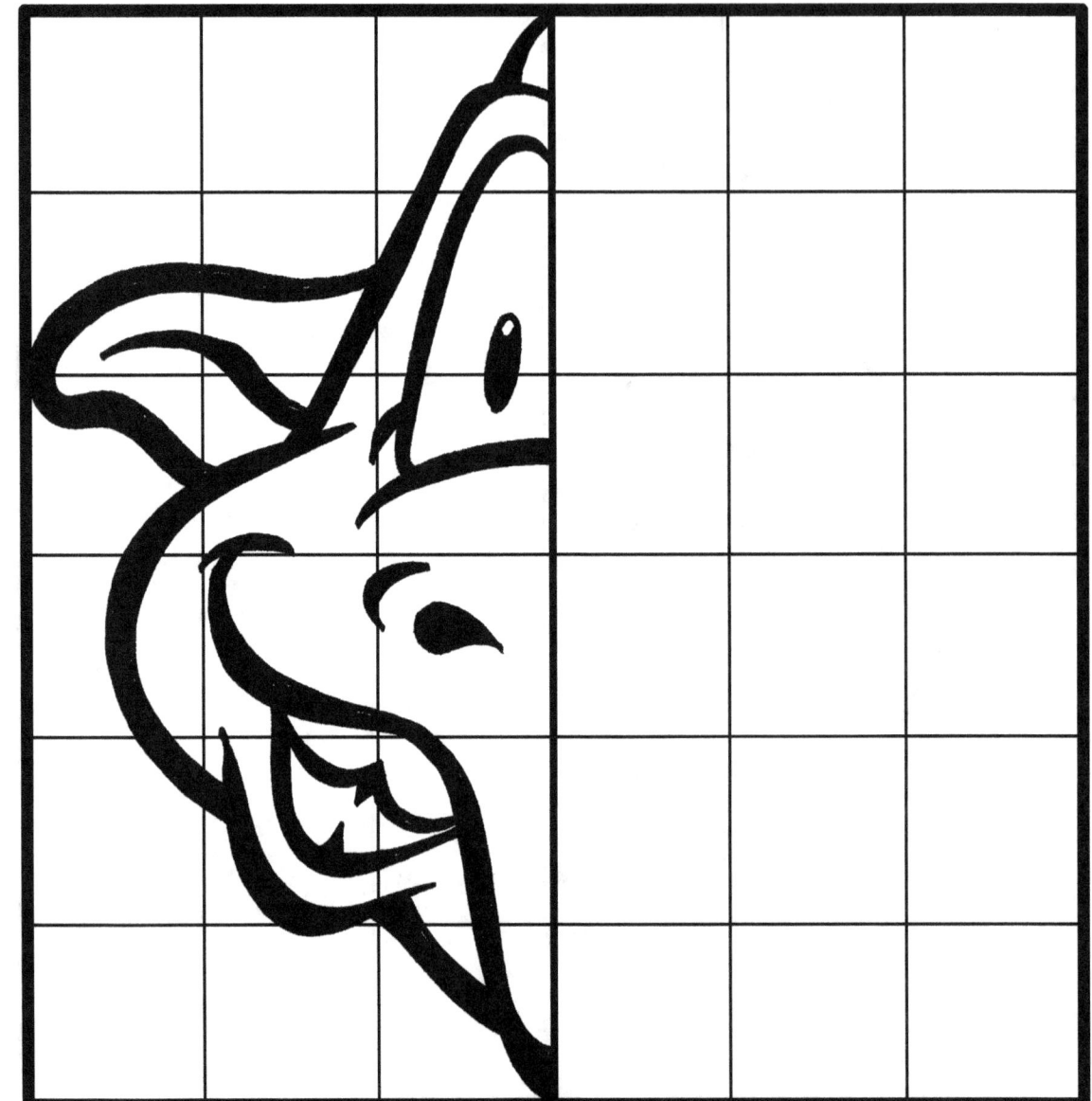

SCHNOZZ

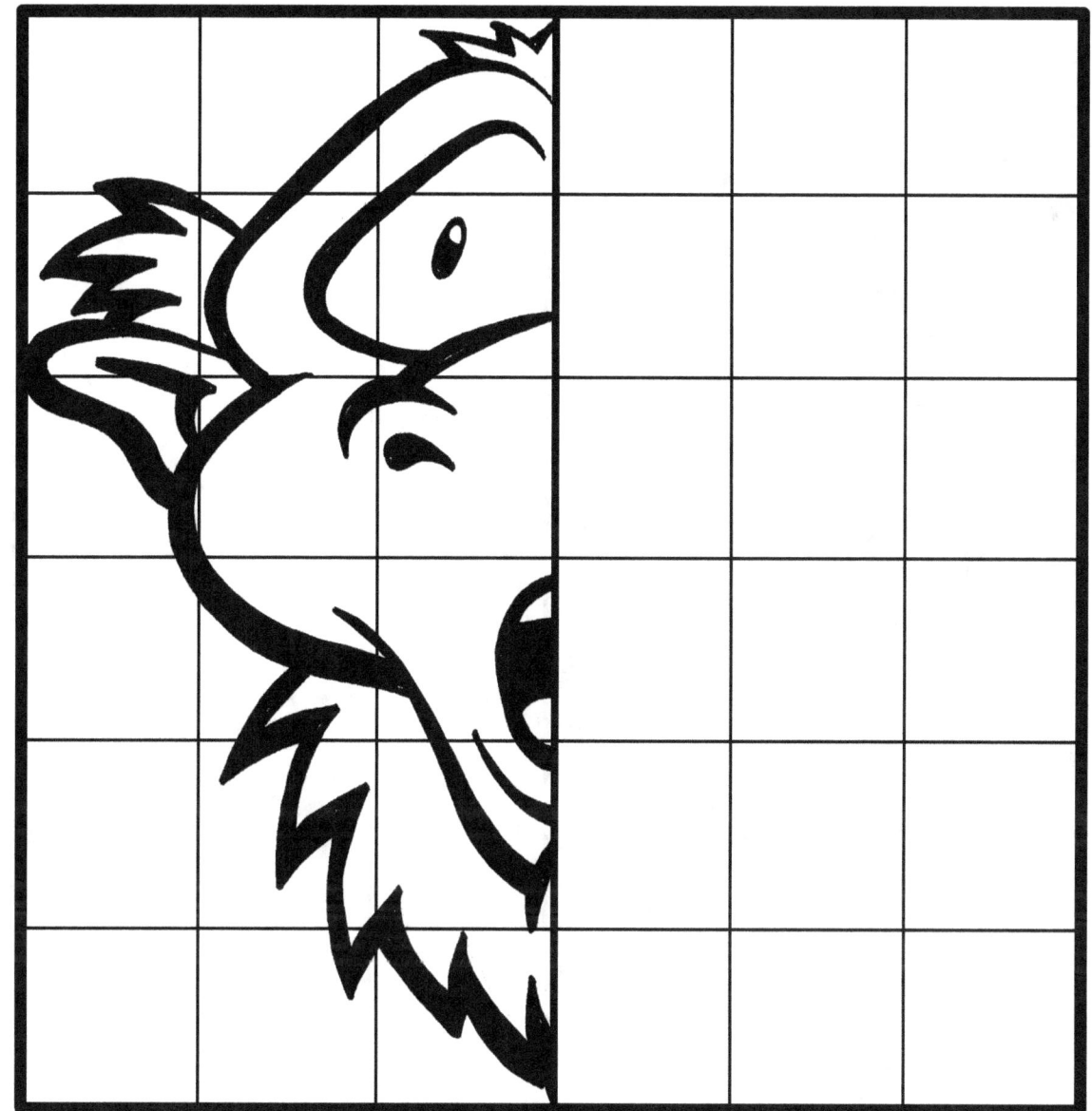

GLOBOO

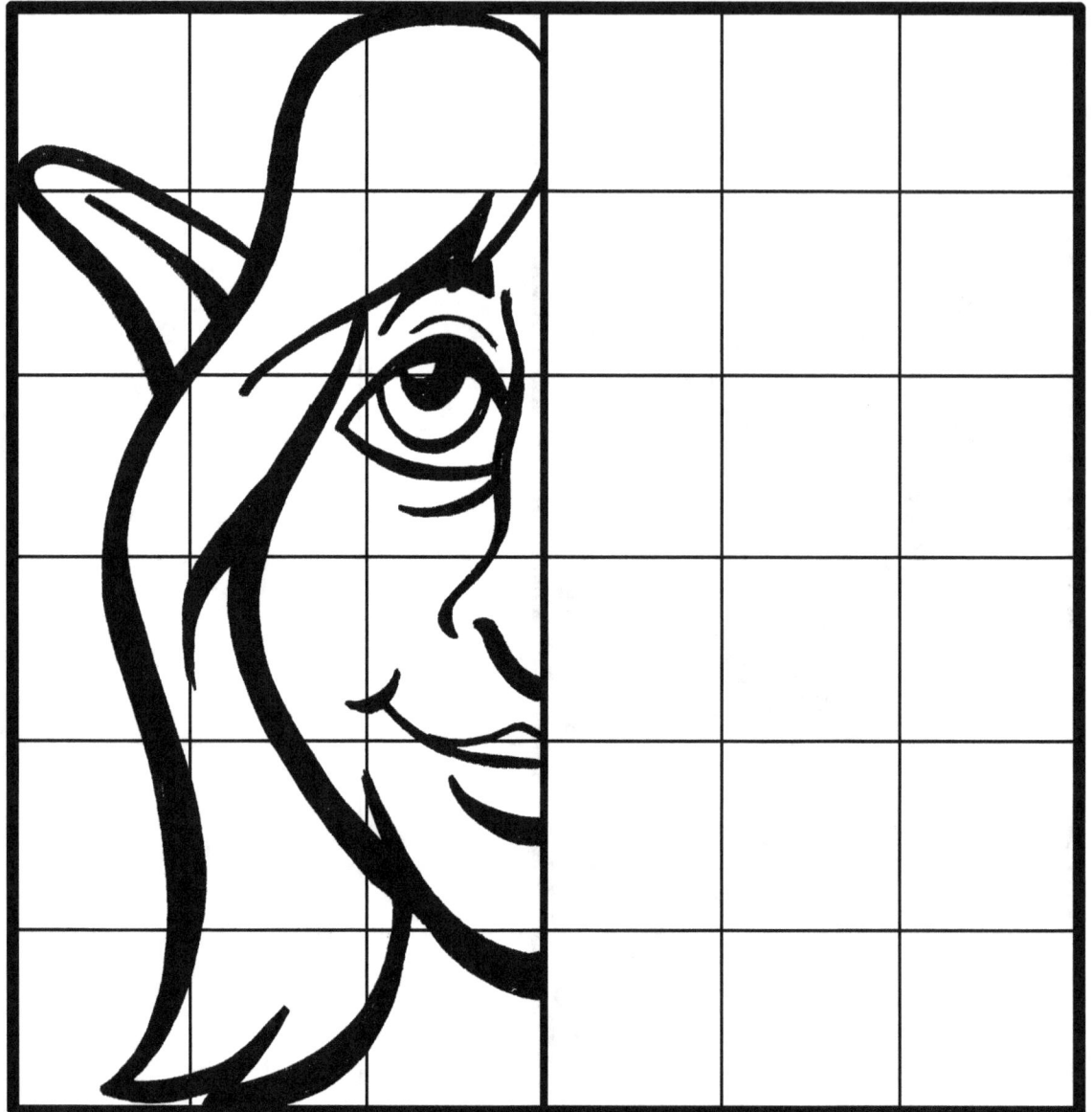

EGGOLASS

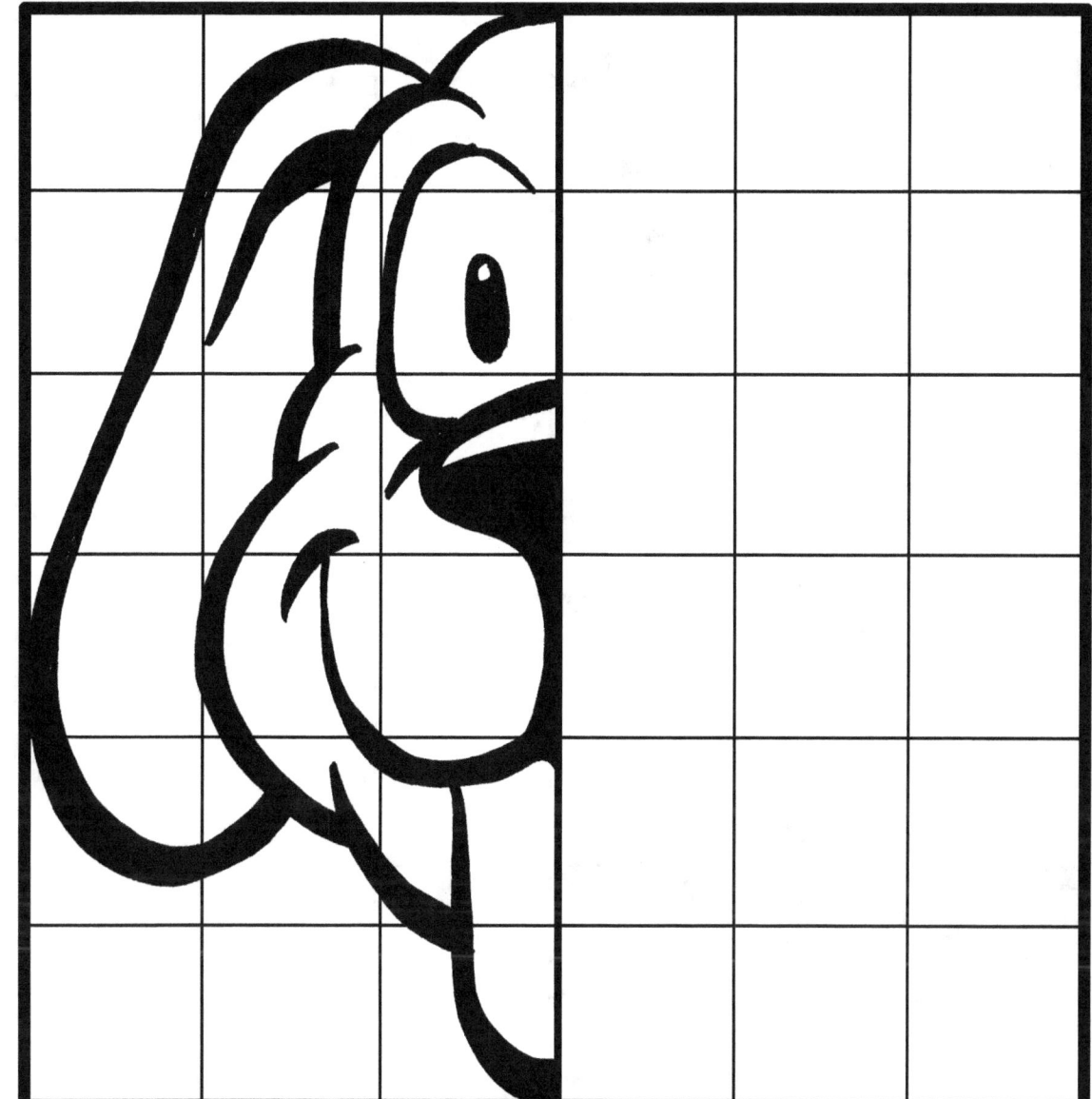

POOCHY

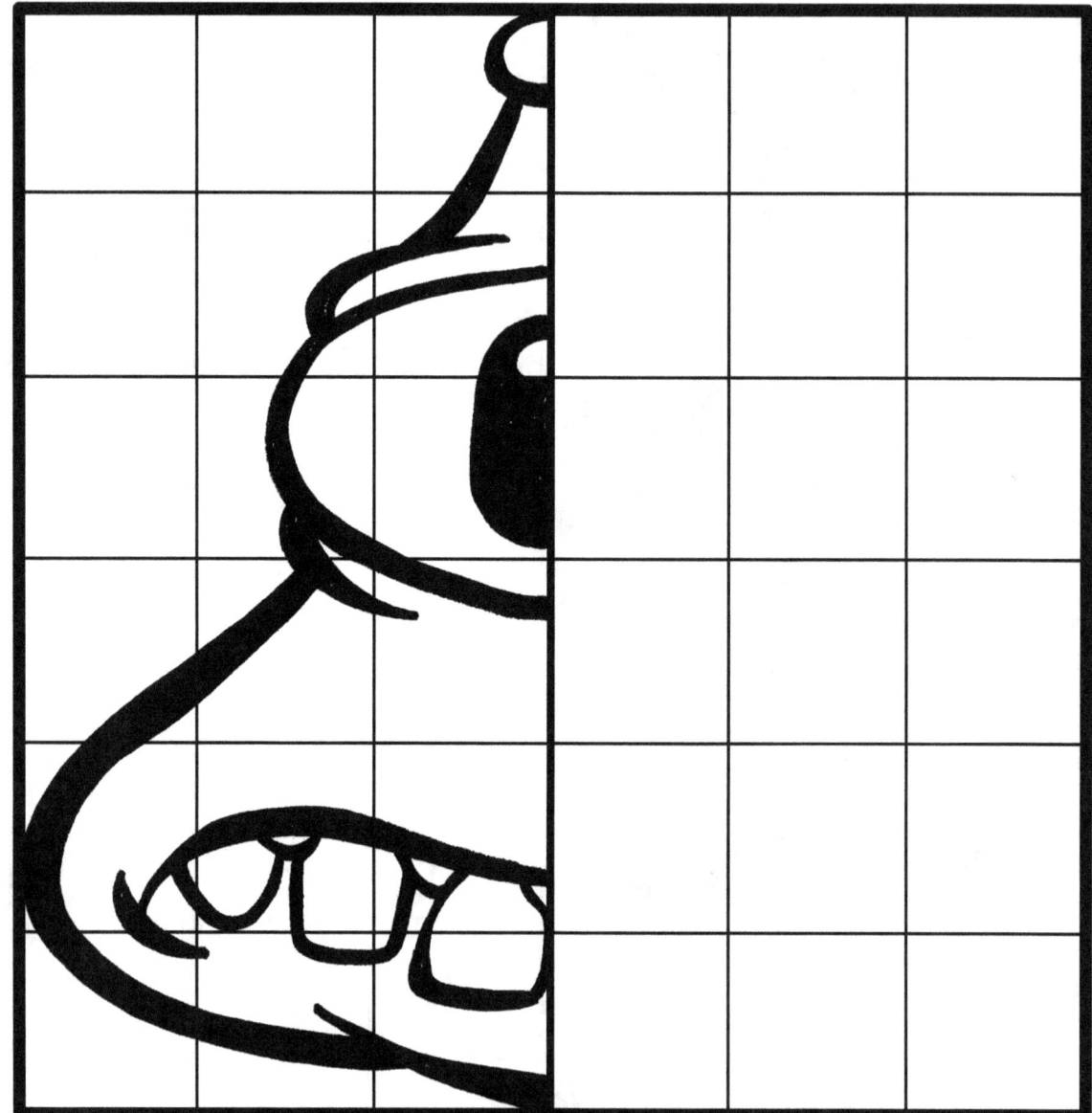

CYCLO

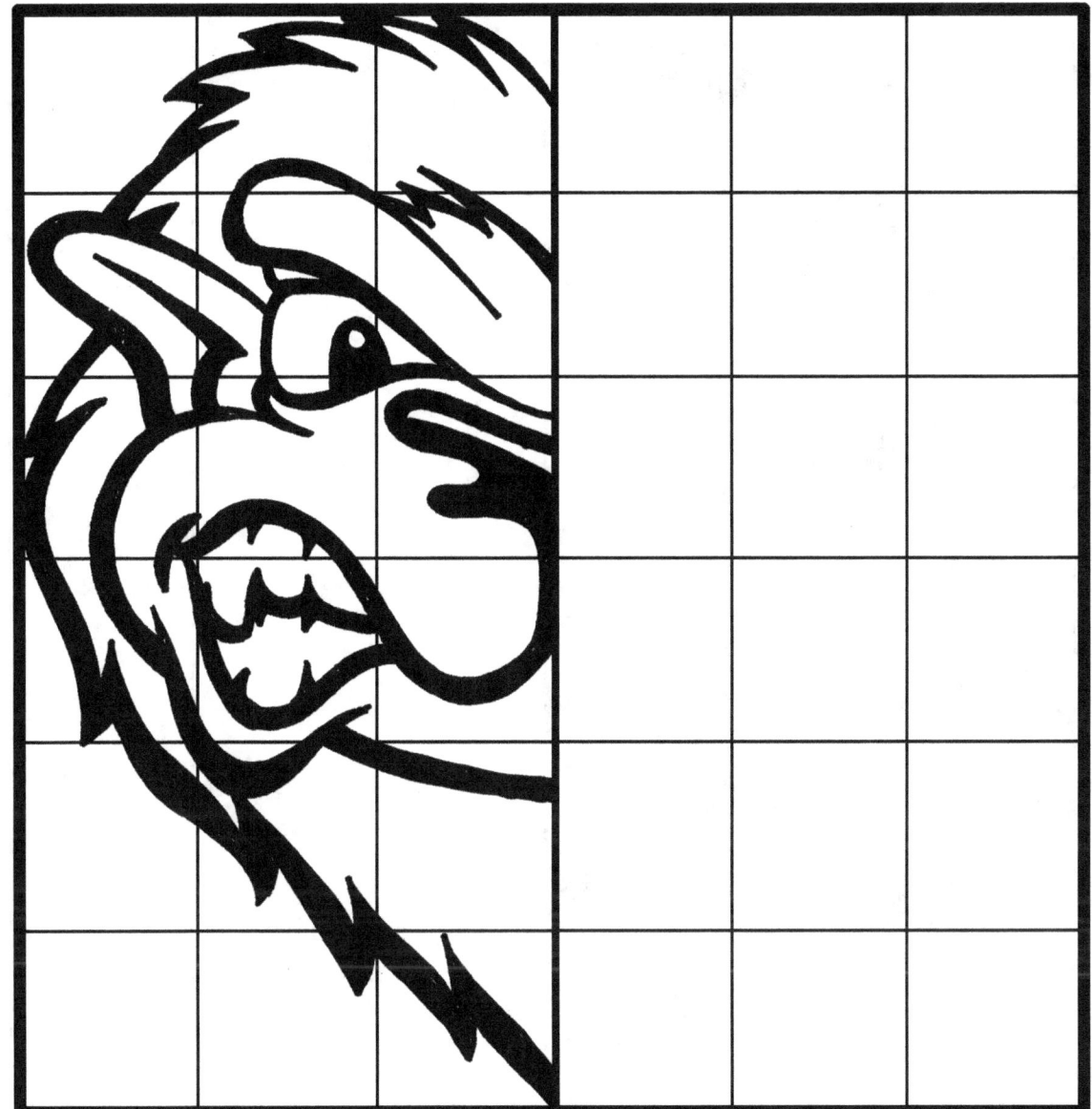

WOLFENSTEIN

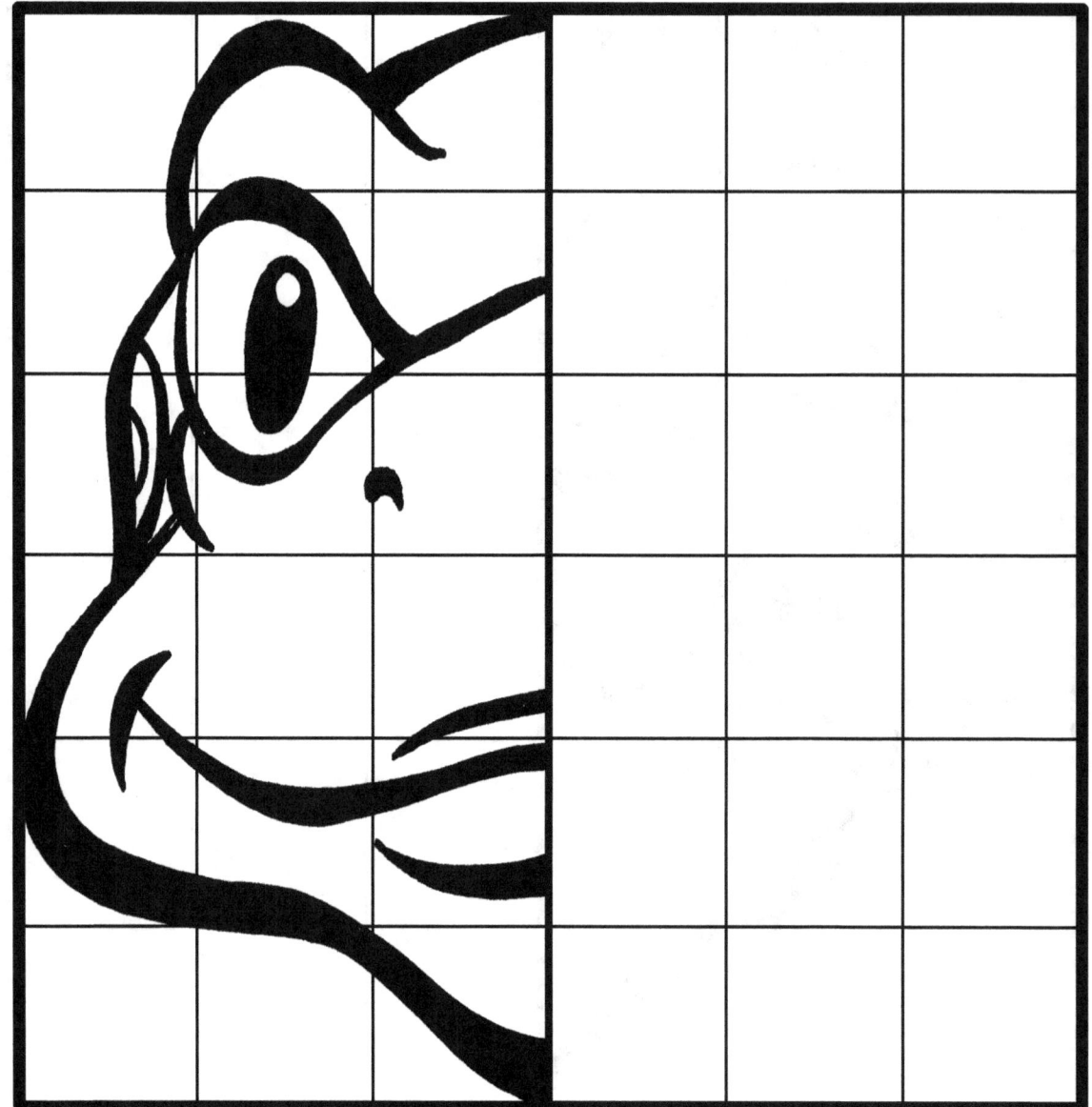

FROSCH

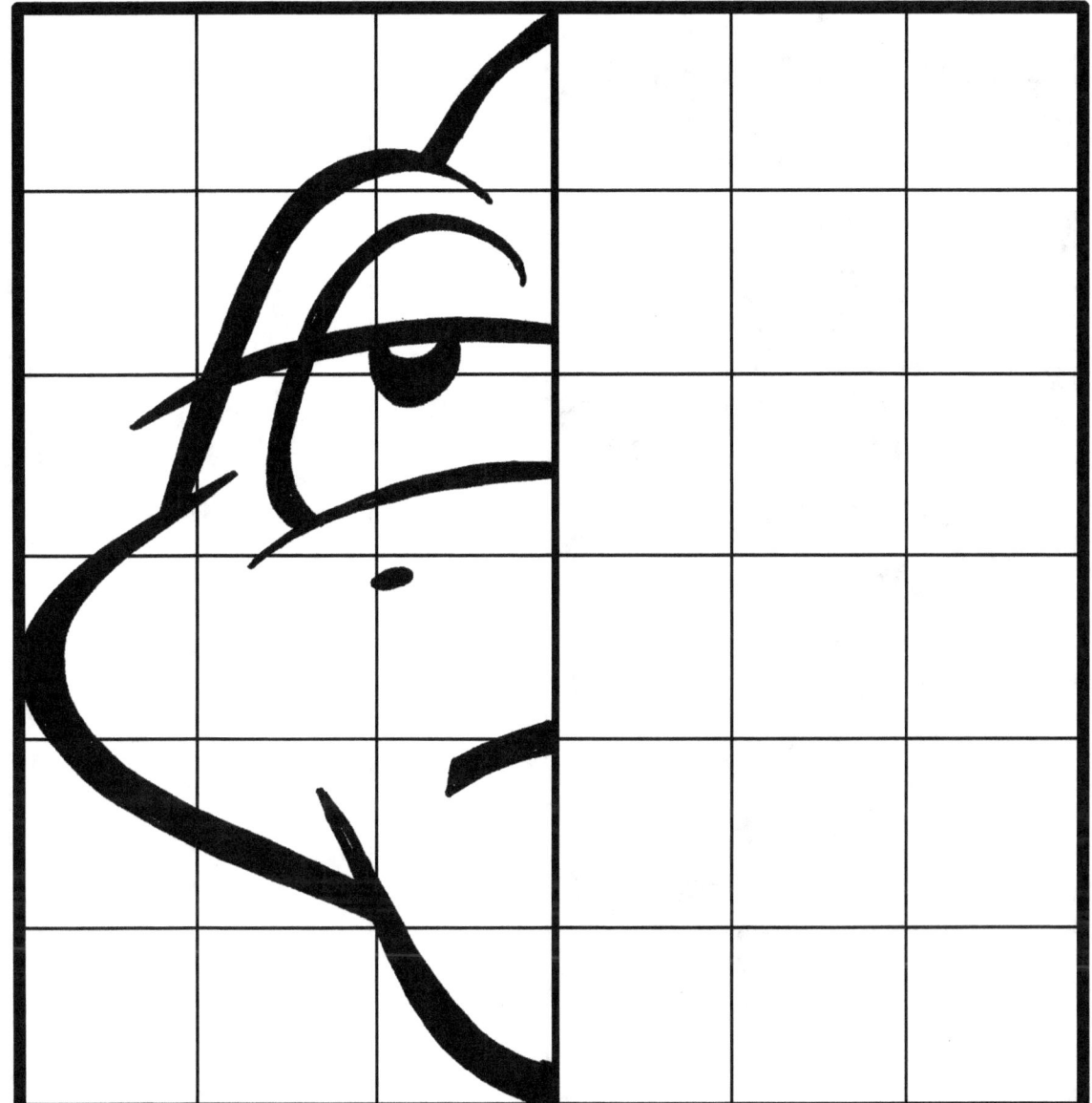

BOREDUMB

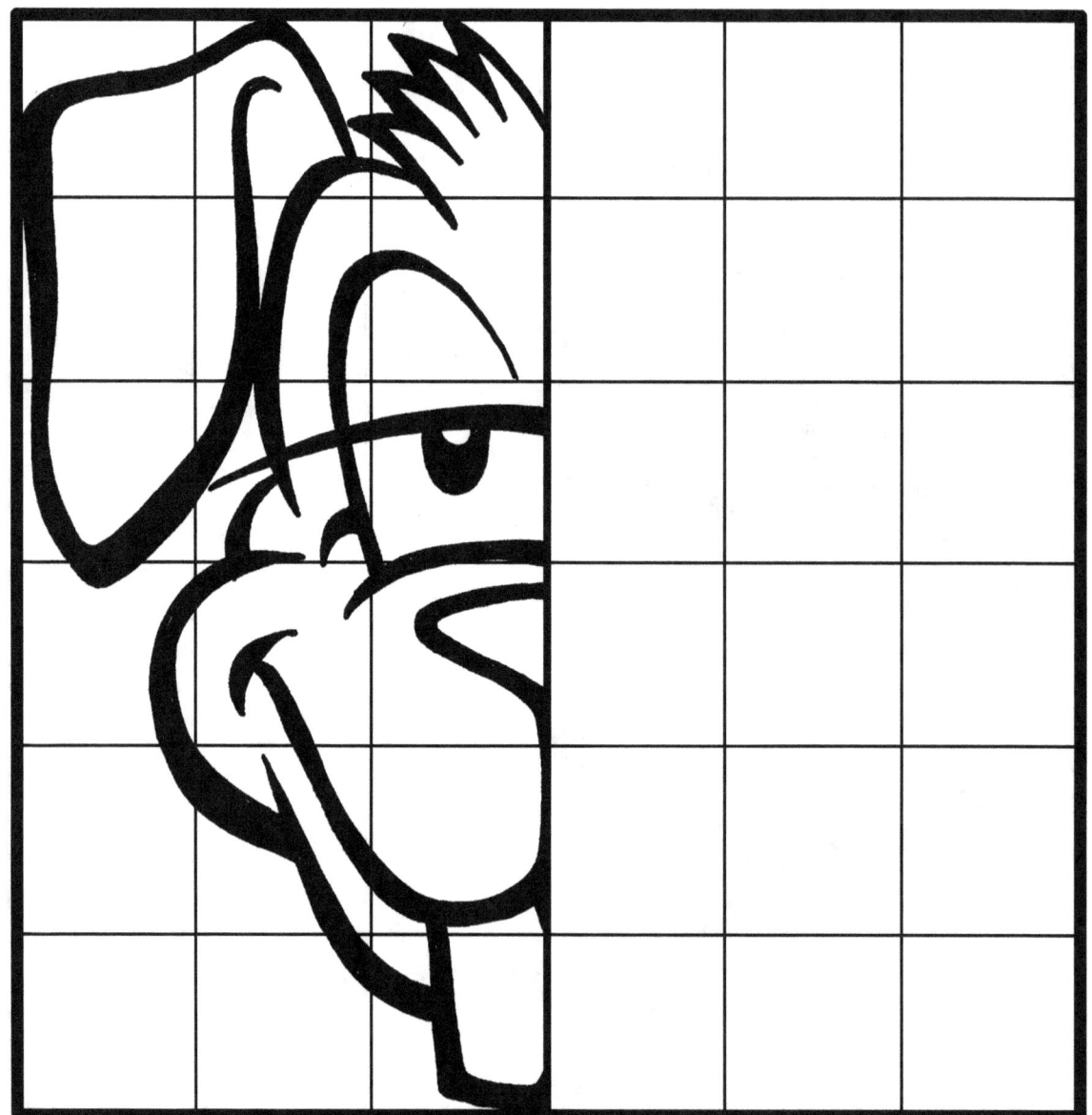

HOPPITY

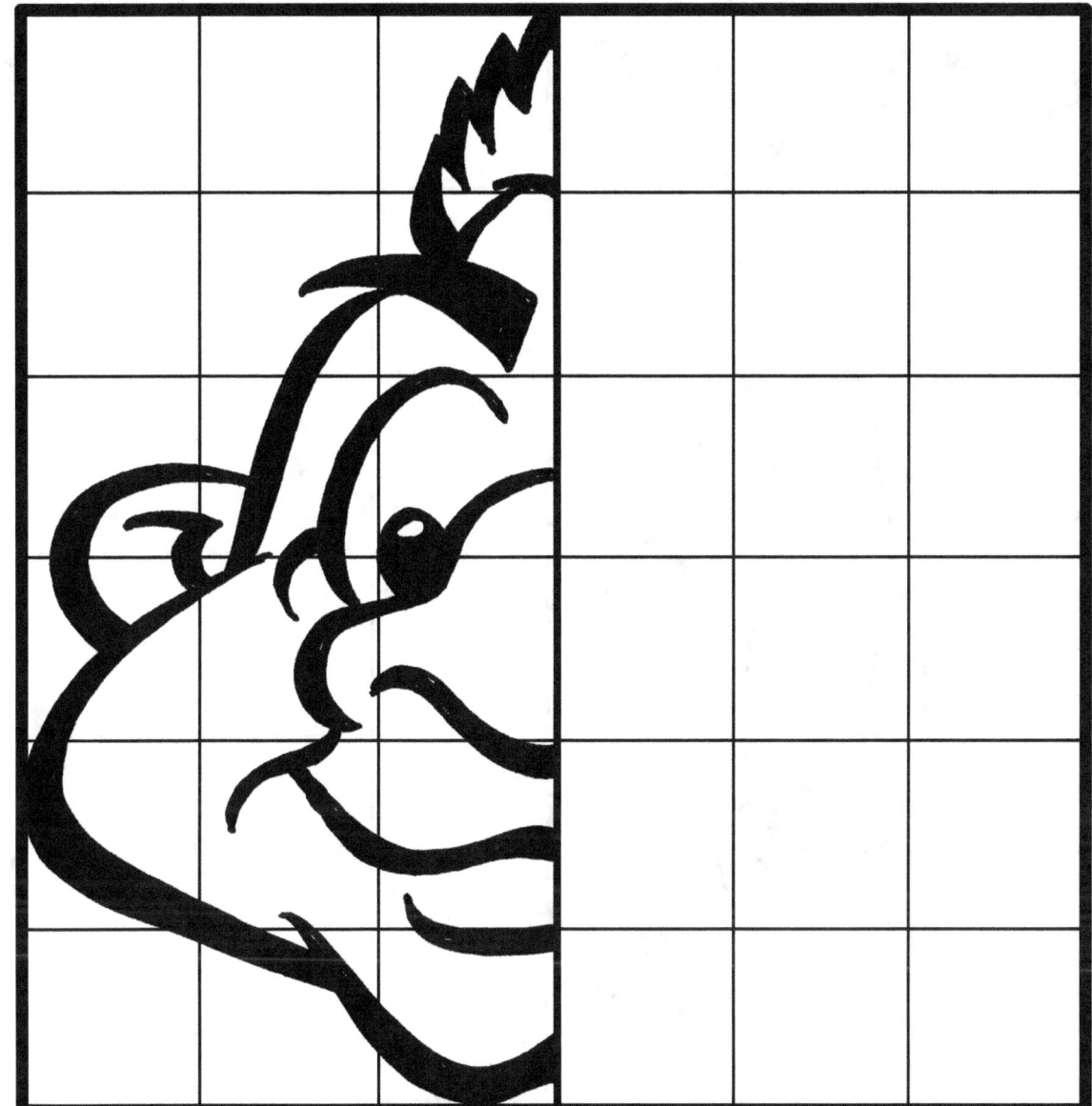

ZIPPIDY

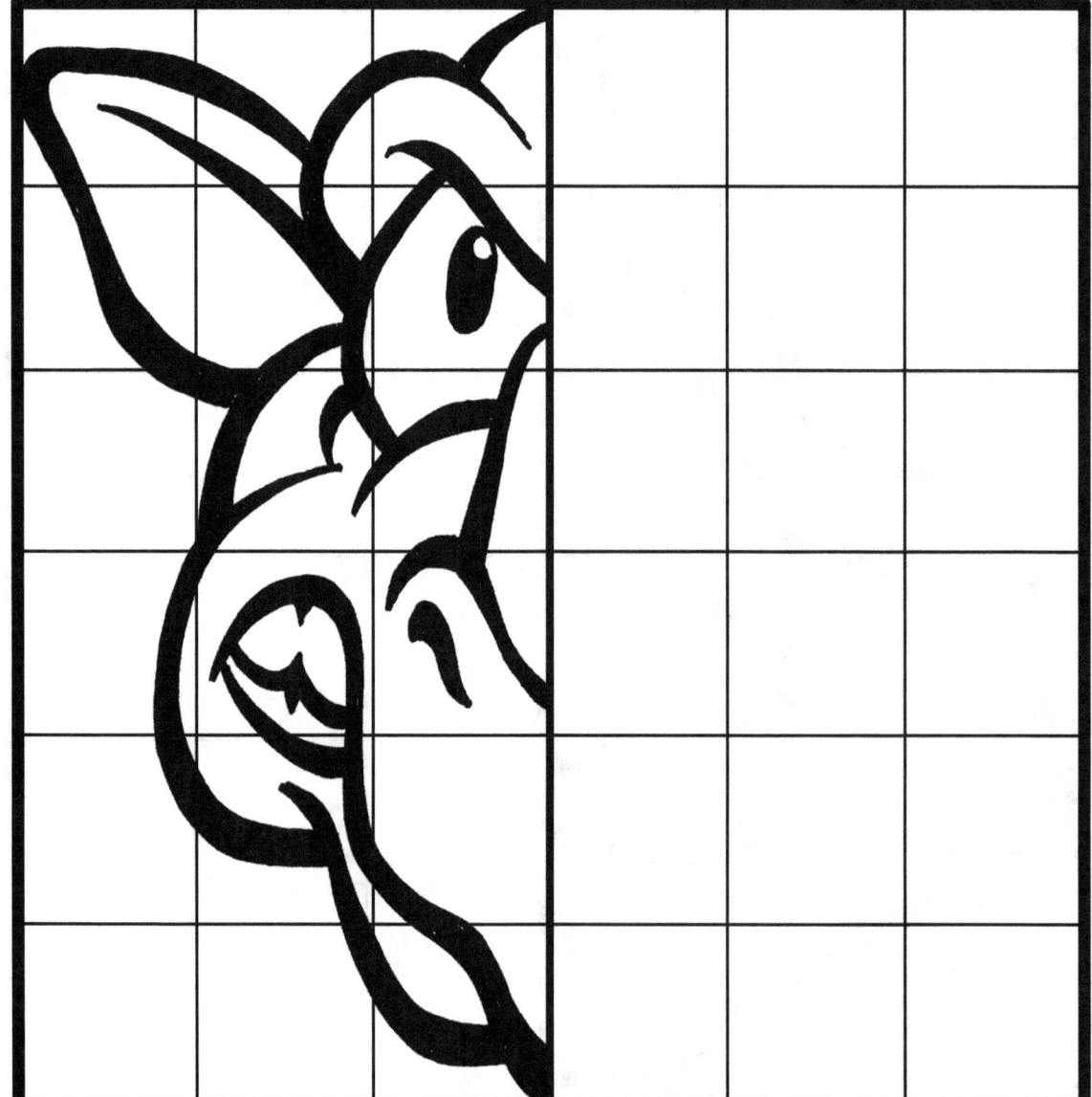

CHARGER

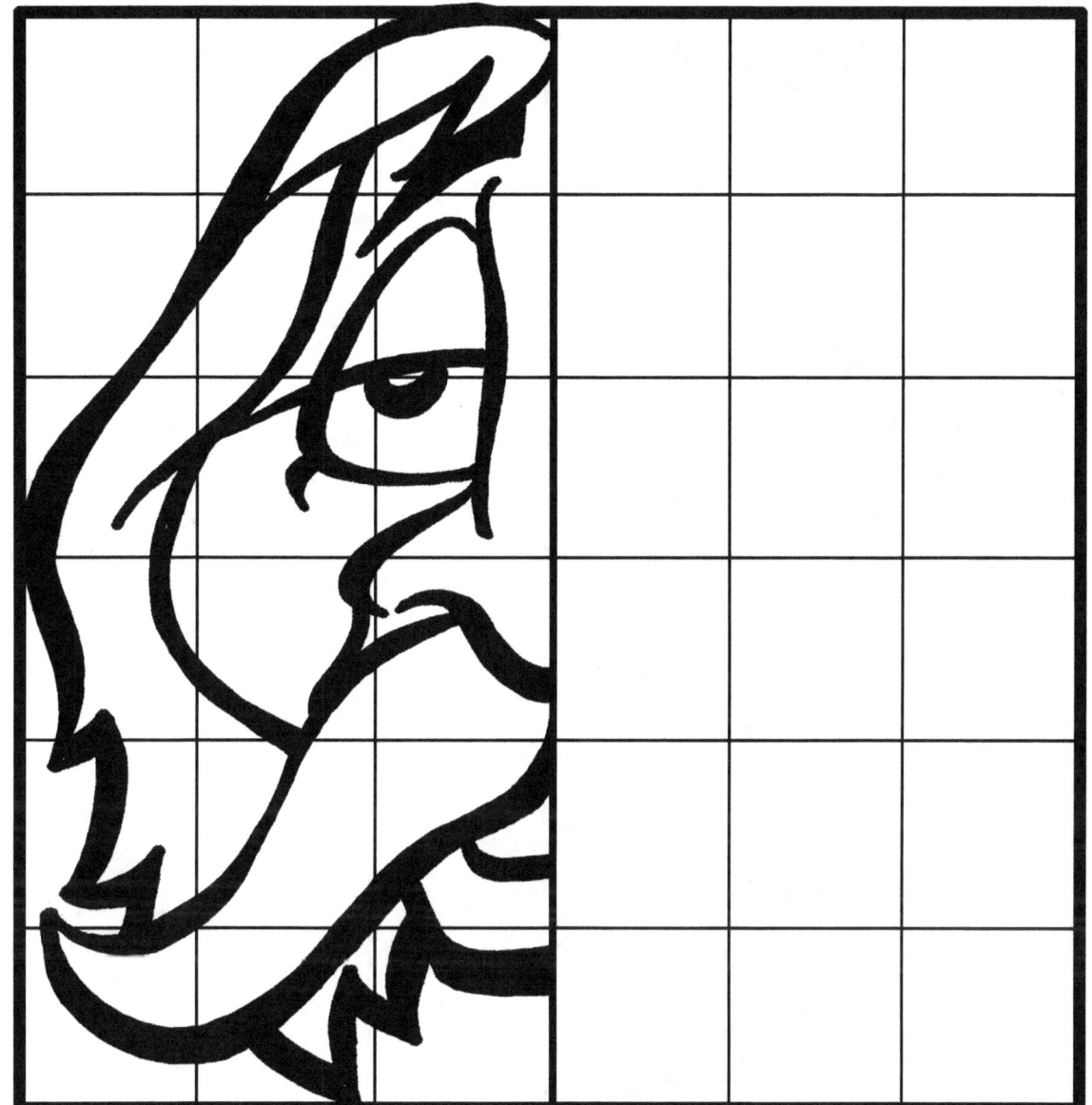

DOC HOLLYDAY

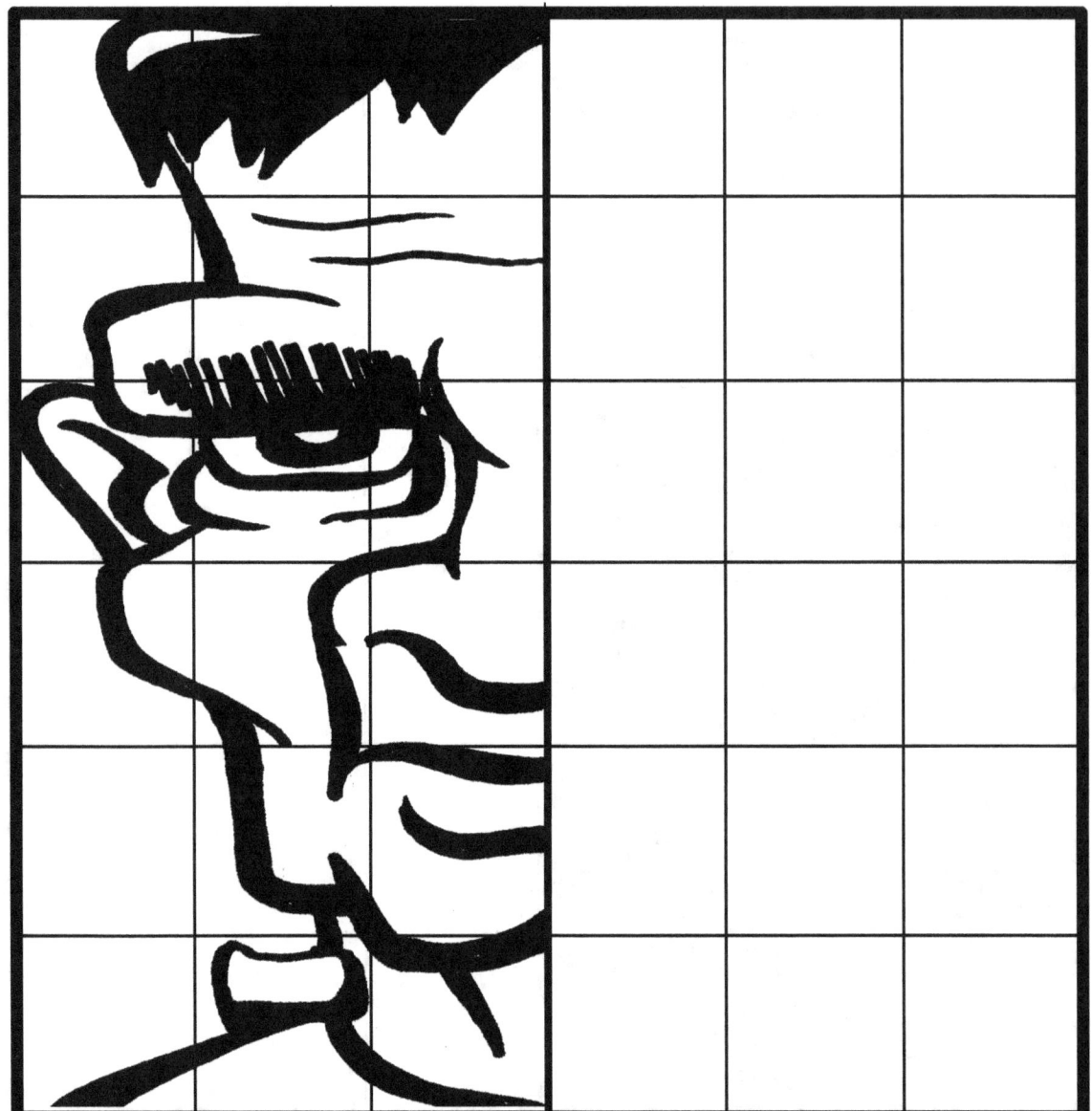

FRANKY-O

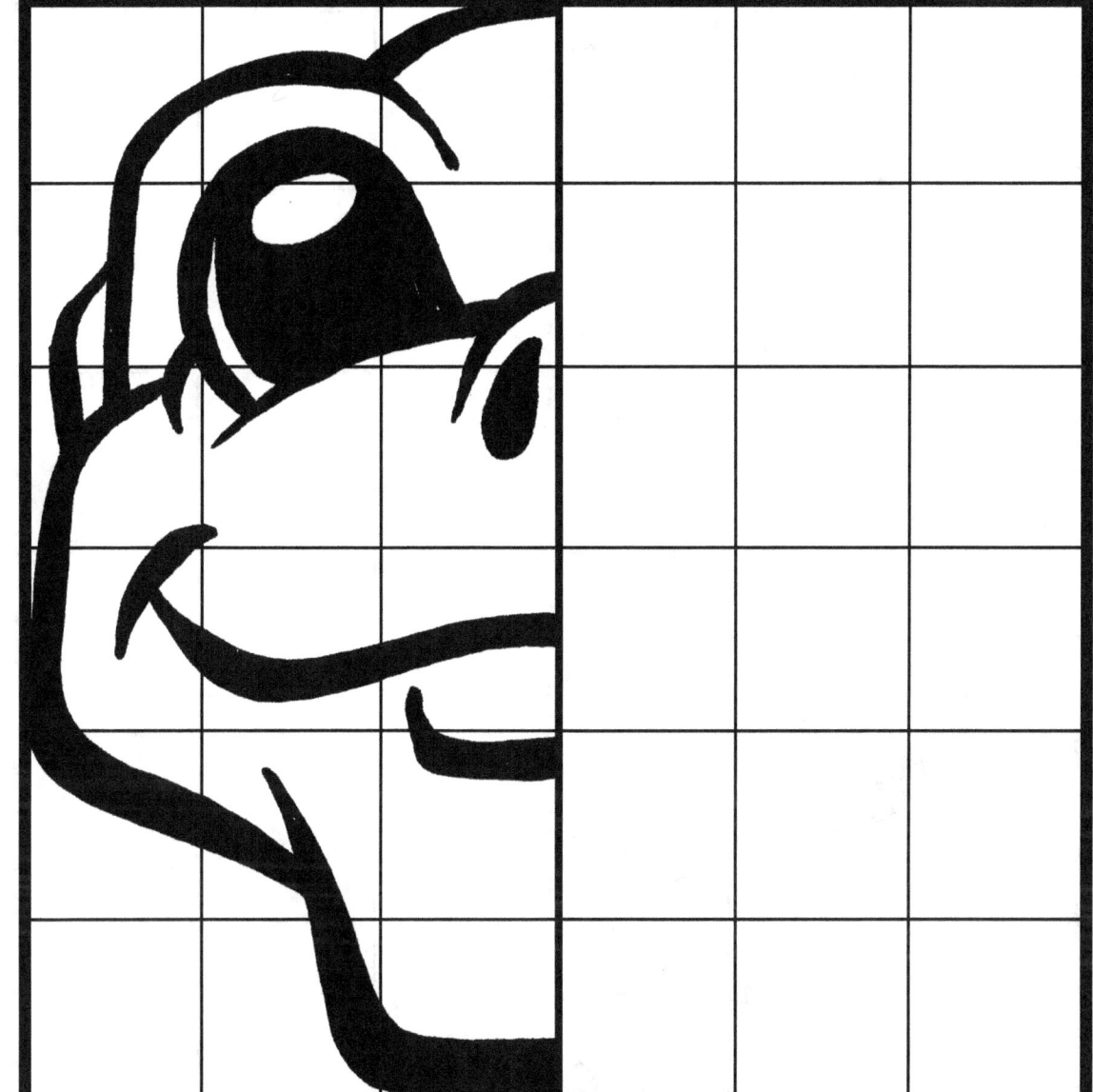

GRAY

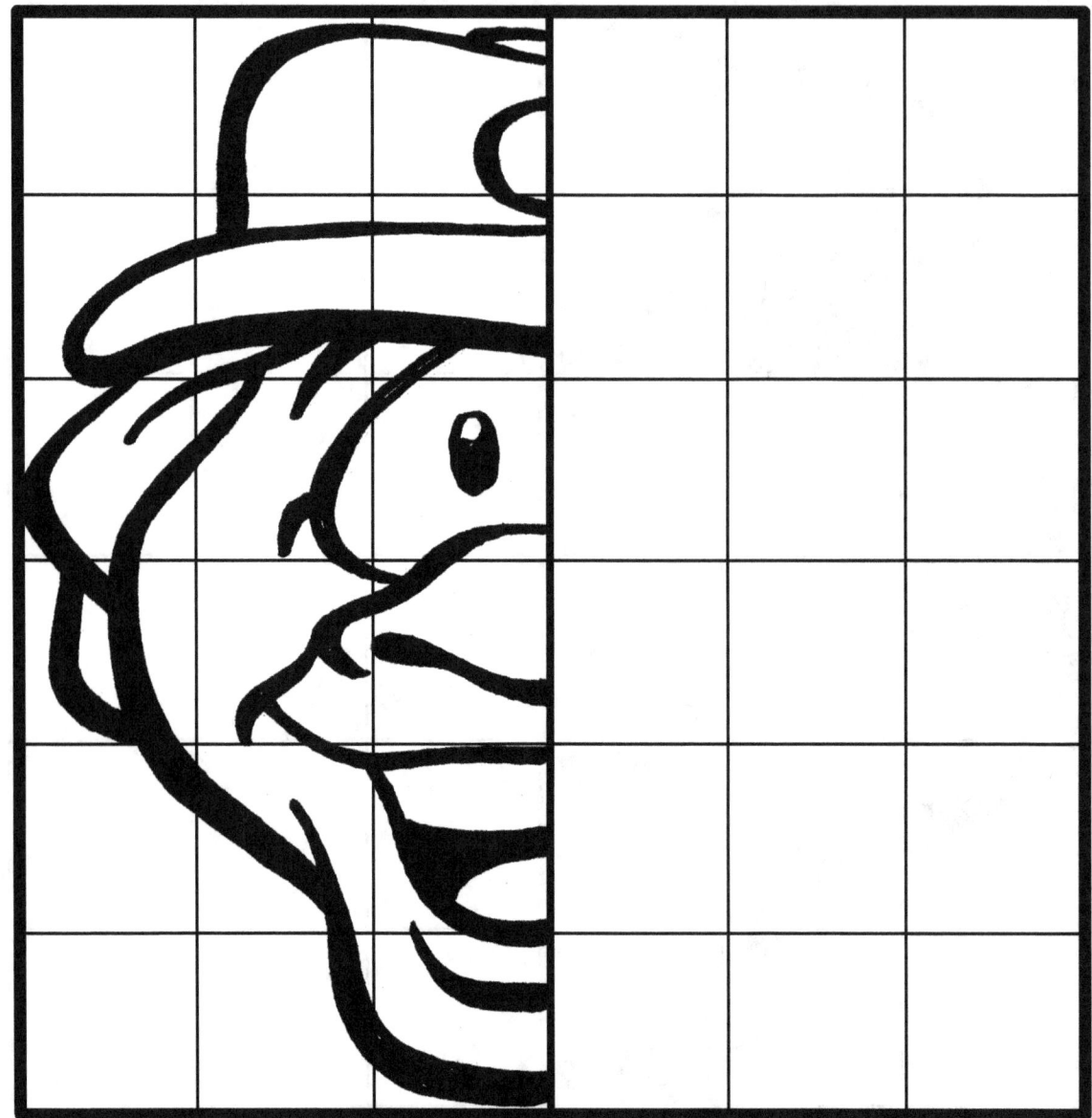

JIM-BOB

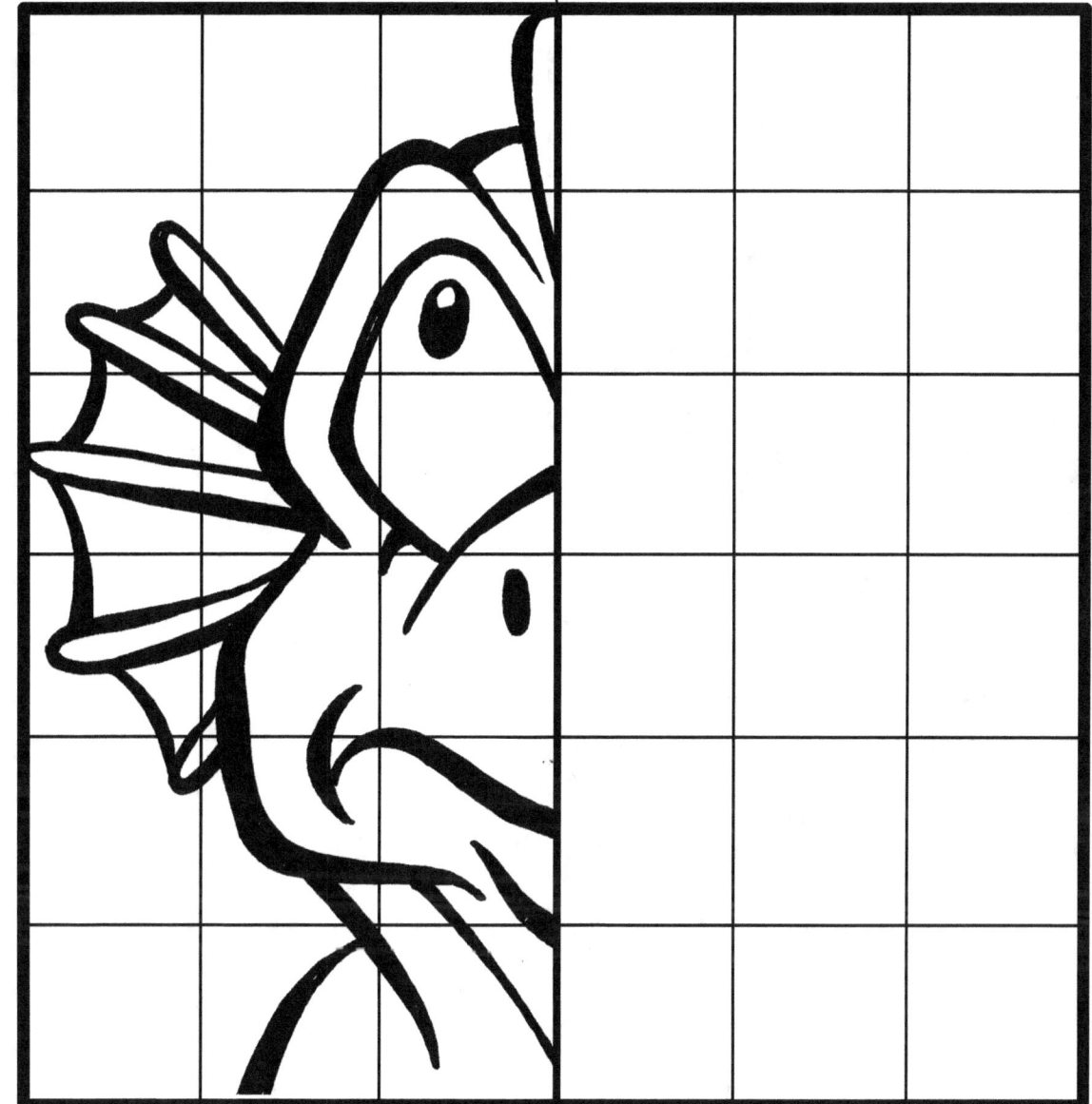

CREECH

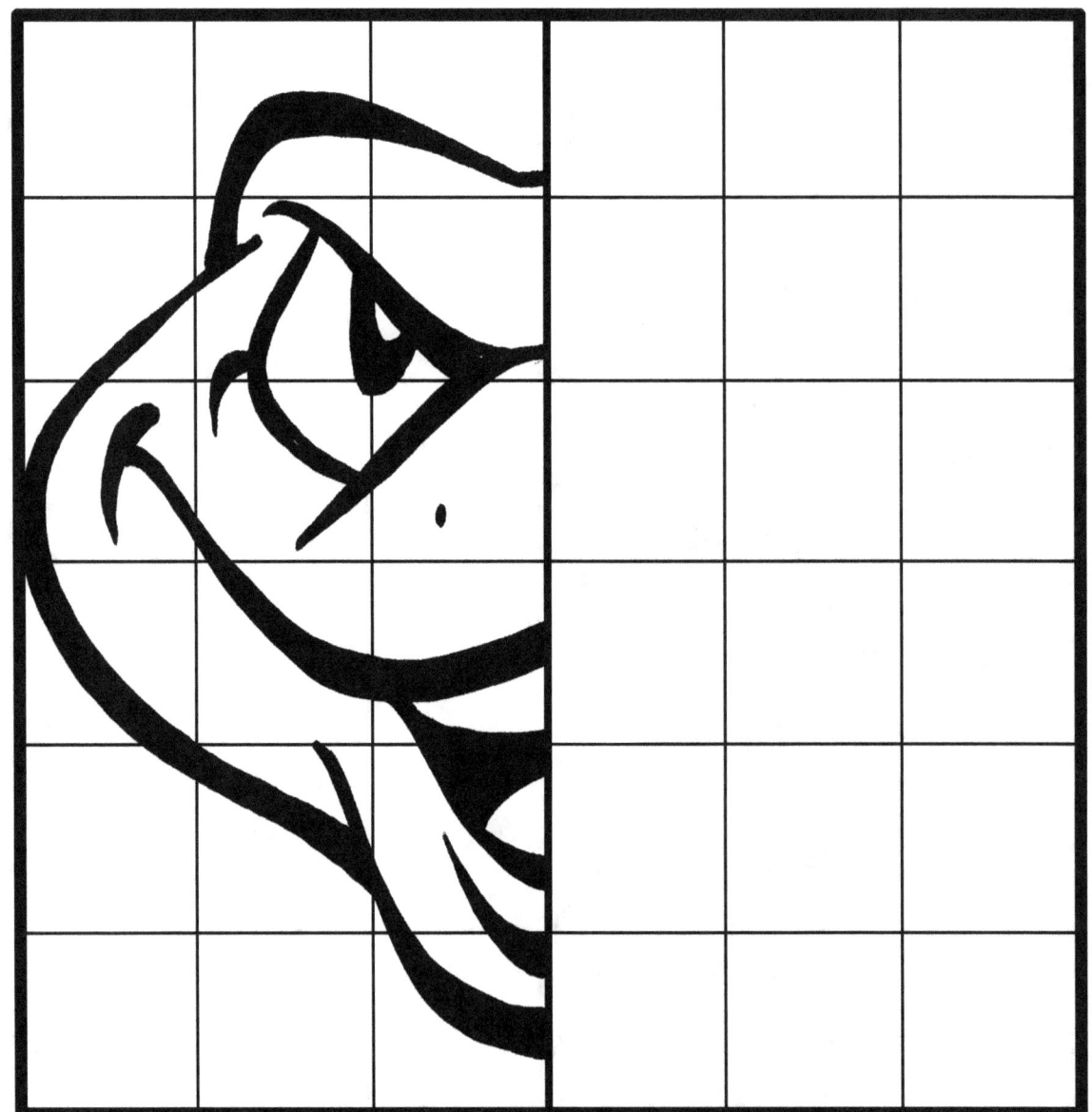

SNARKULOUS

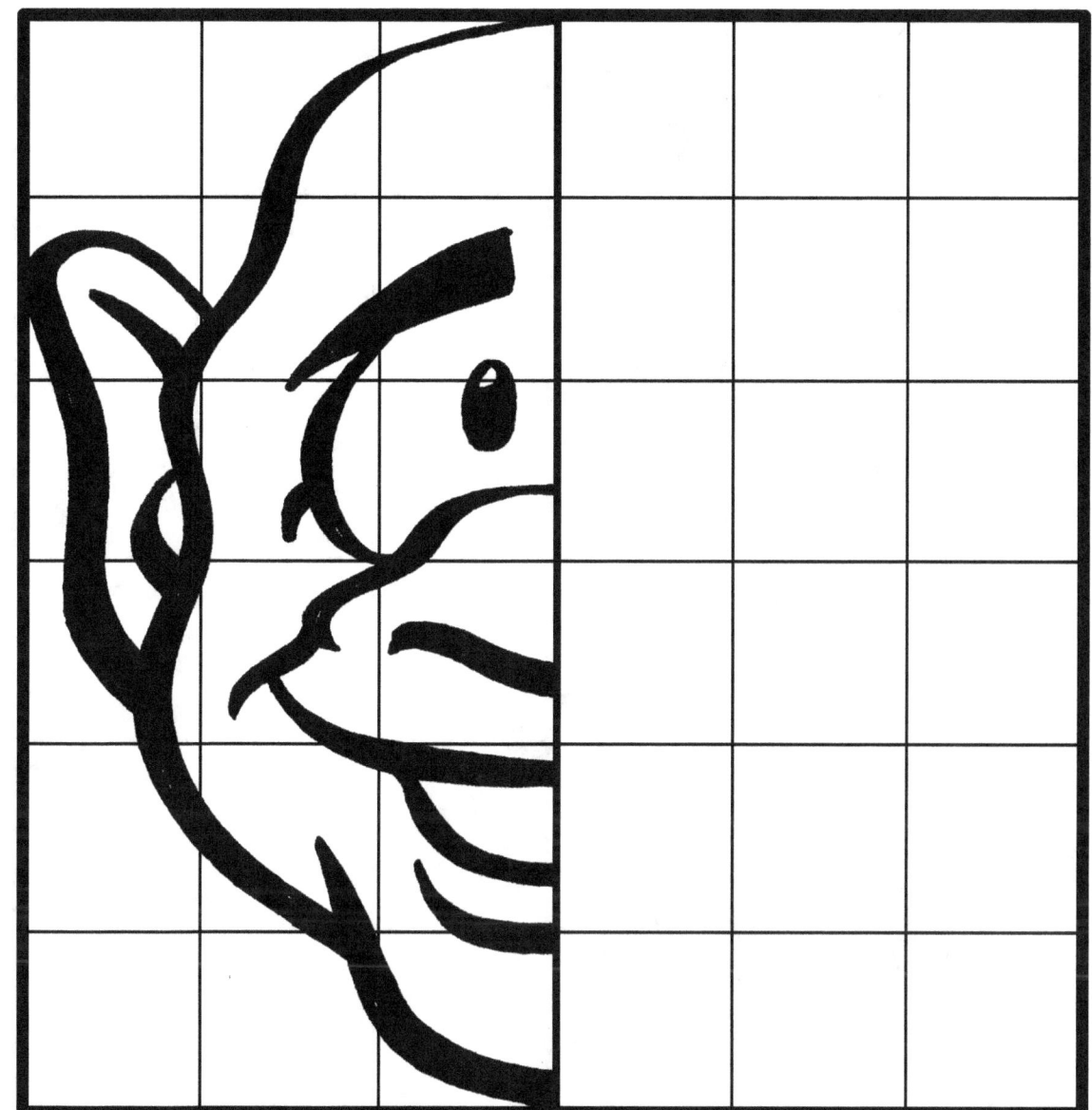

SMILIN' BIFF

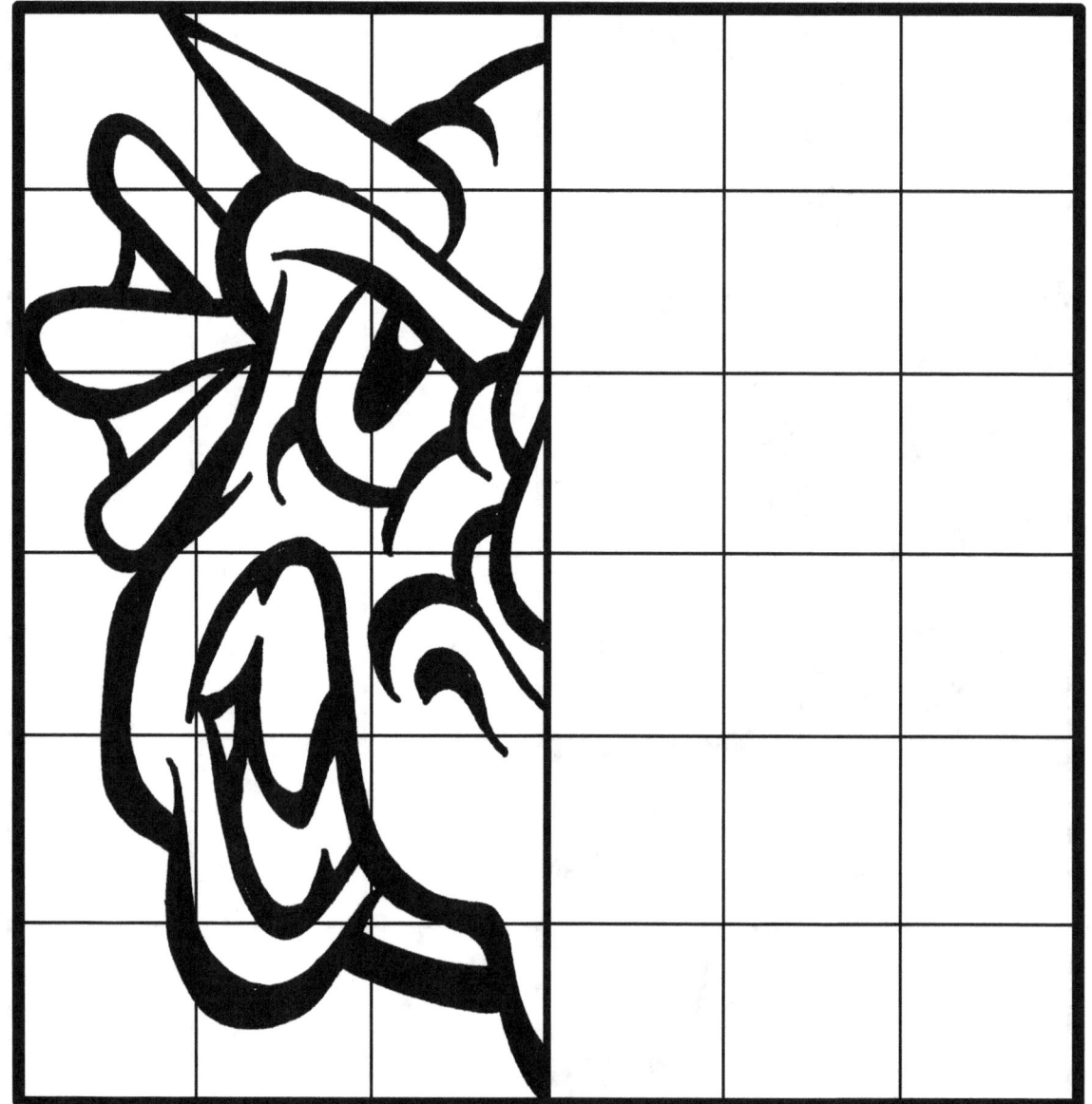

DRACONIAN

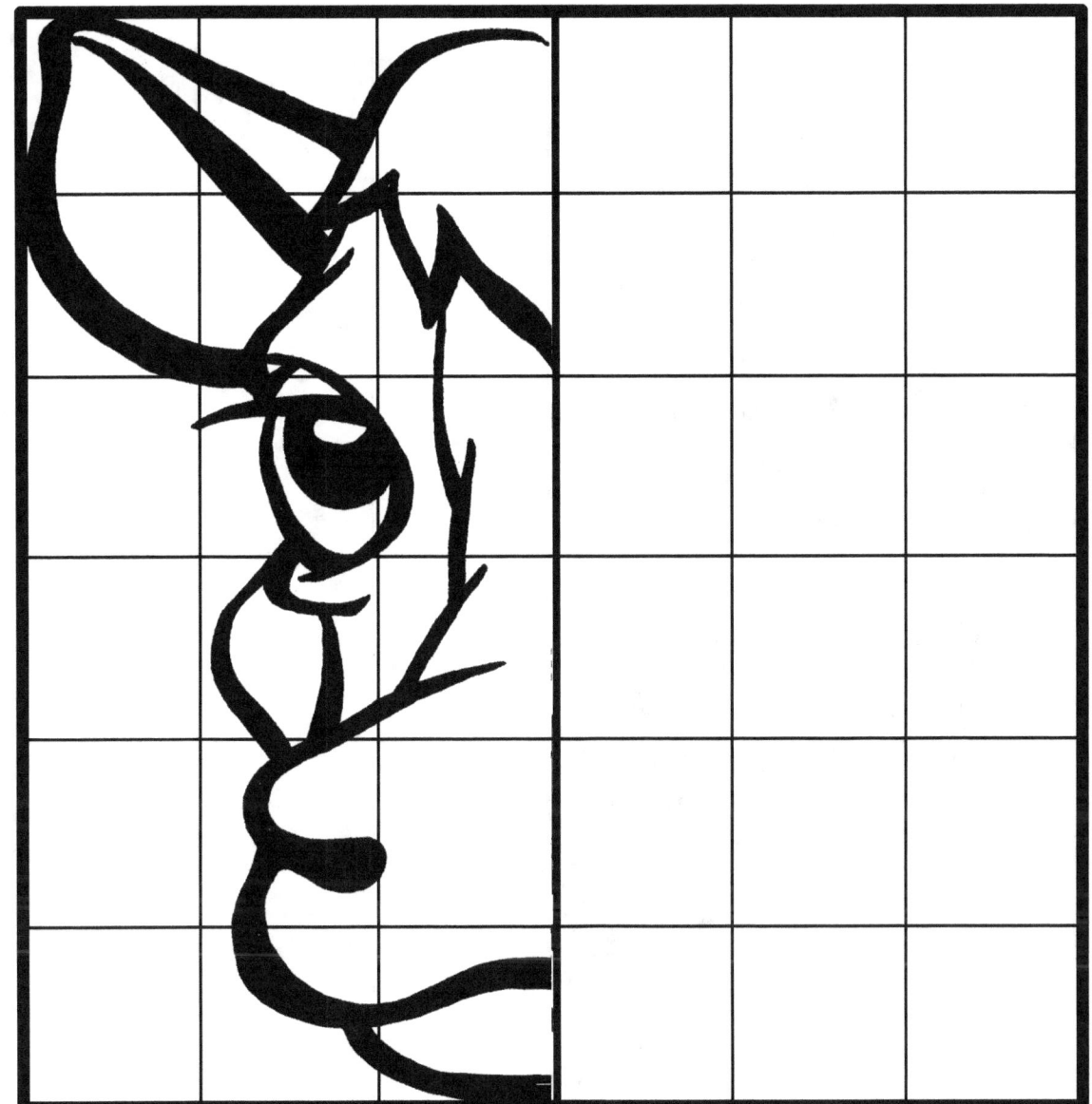

PFRED PFERD

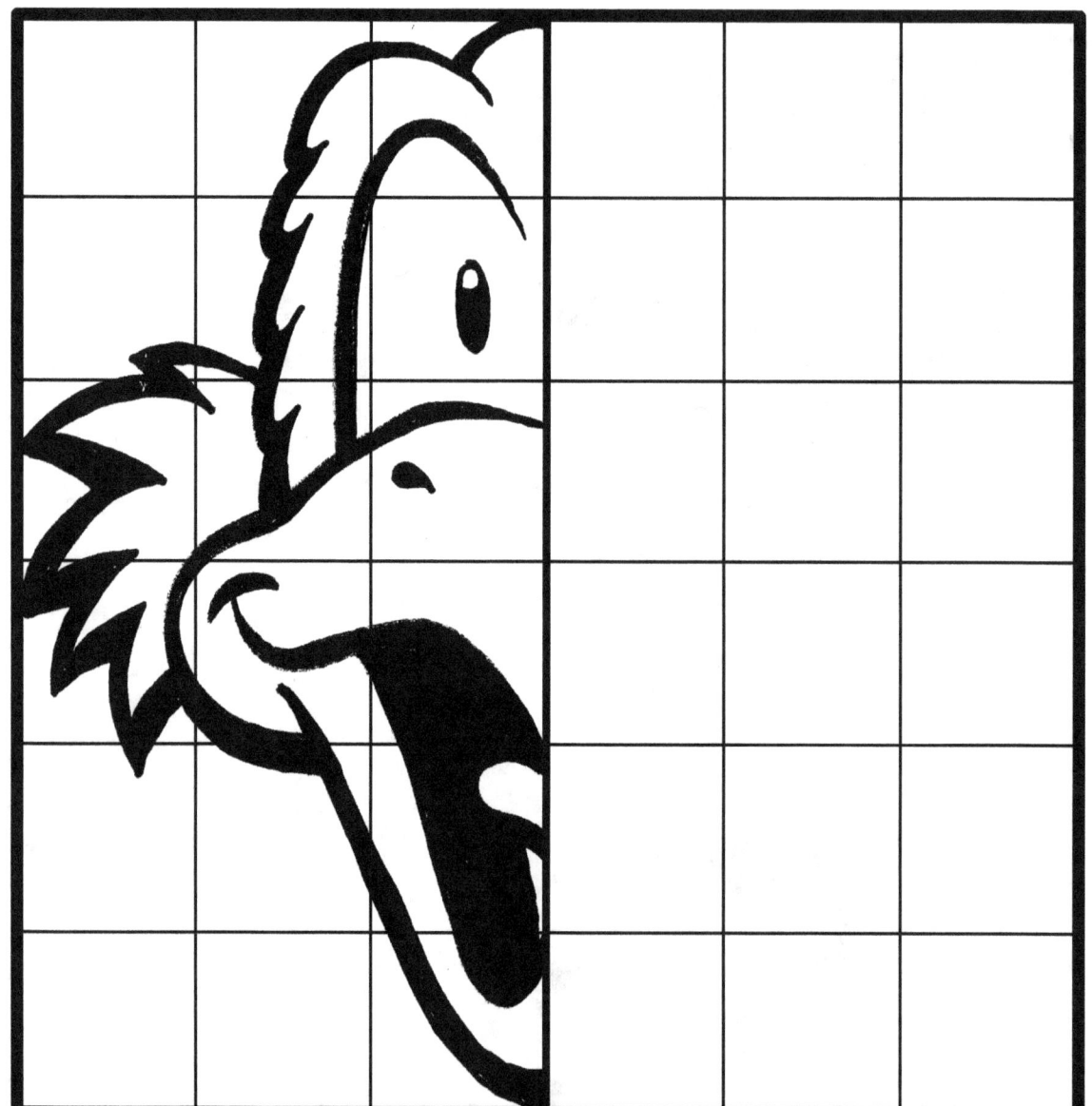

MAGGY PIE

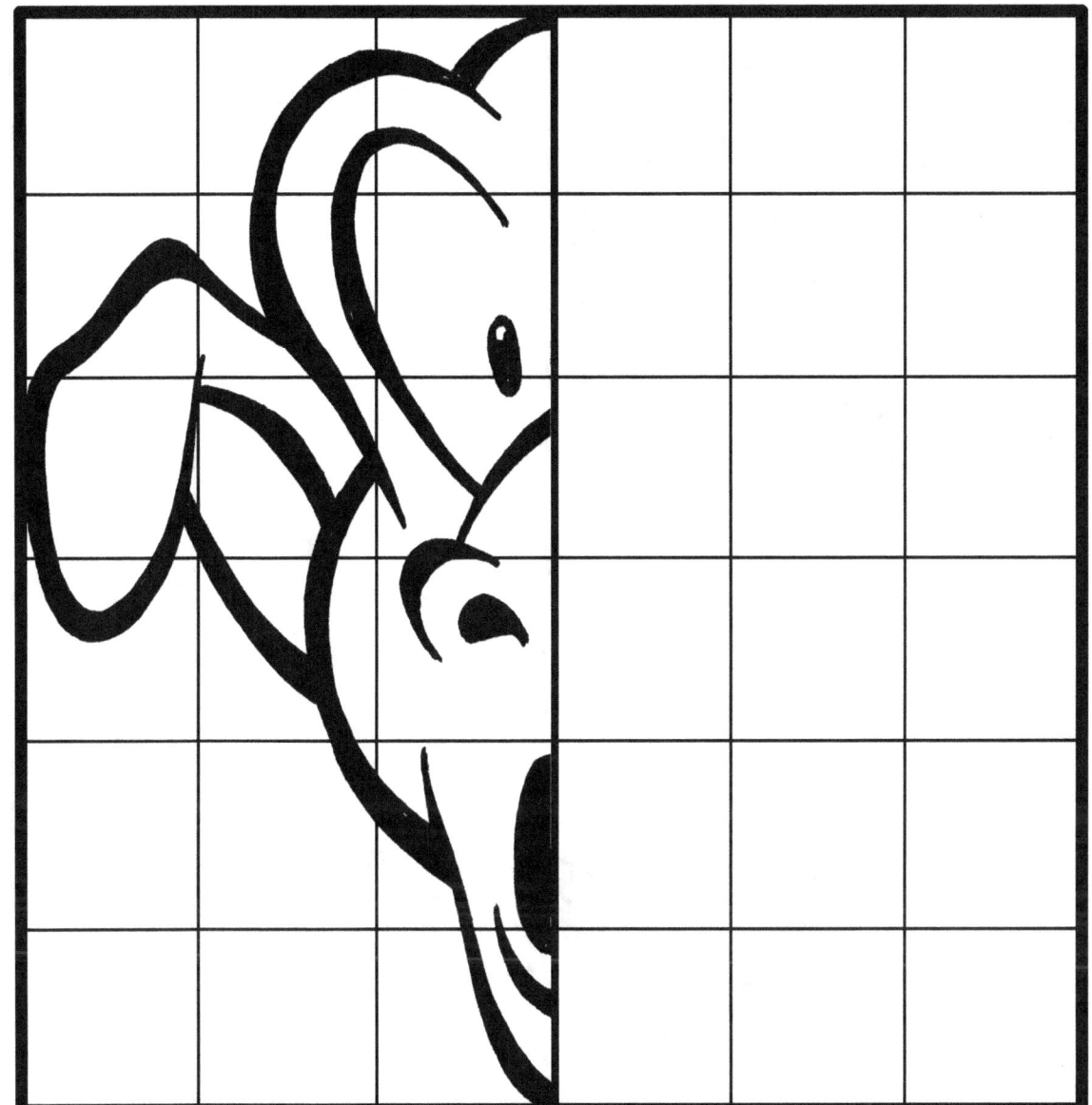

PHREEKOUT

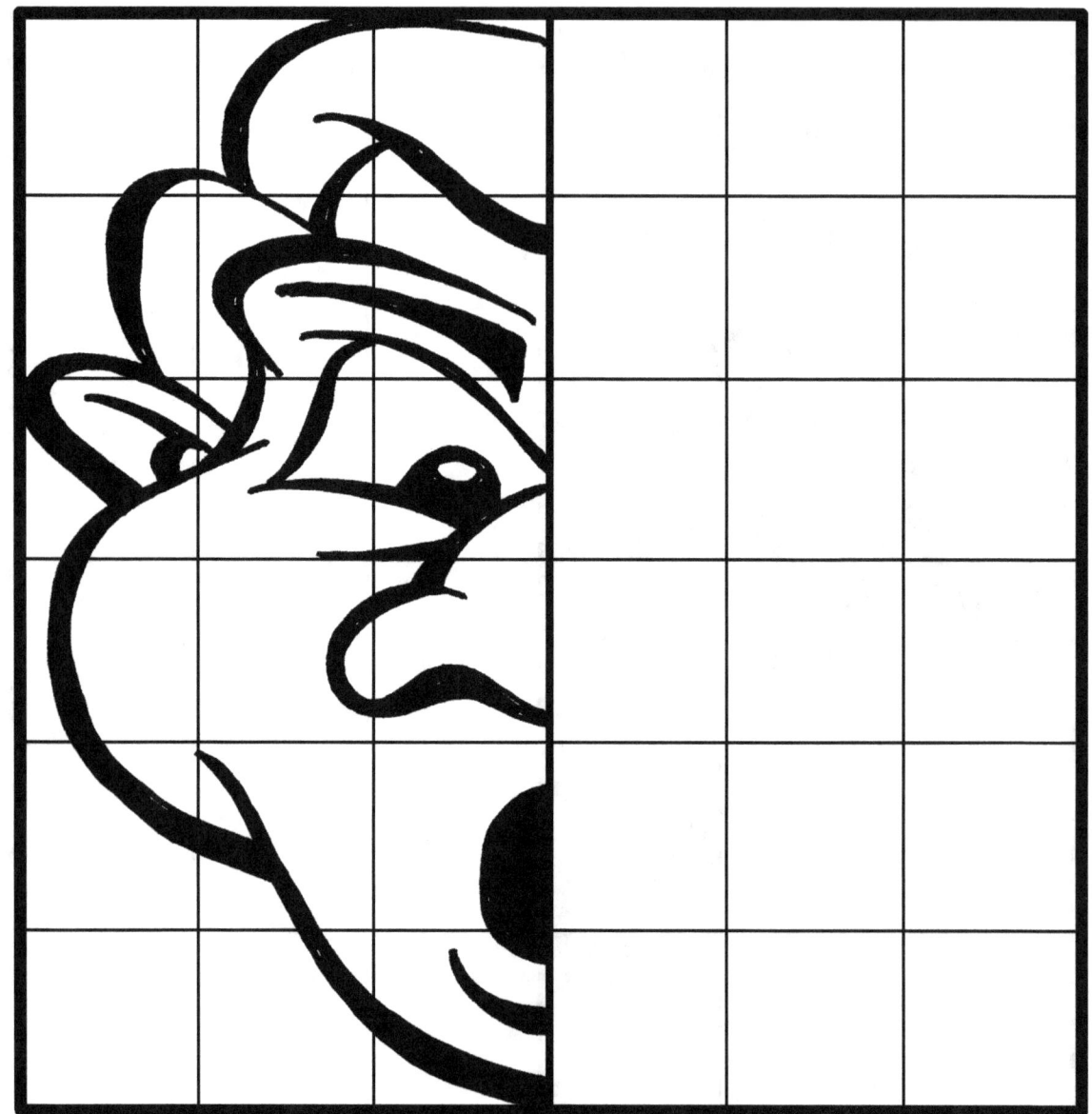

PHLIPPIN' PHIL

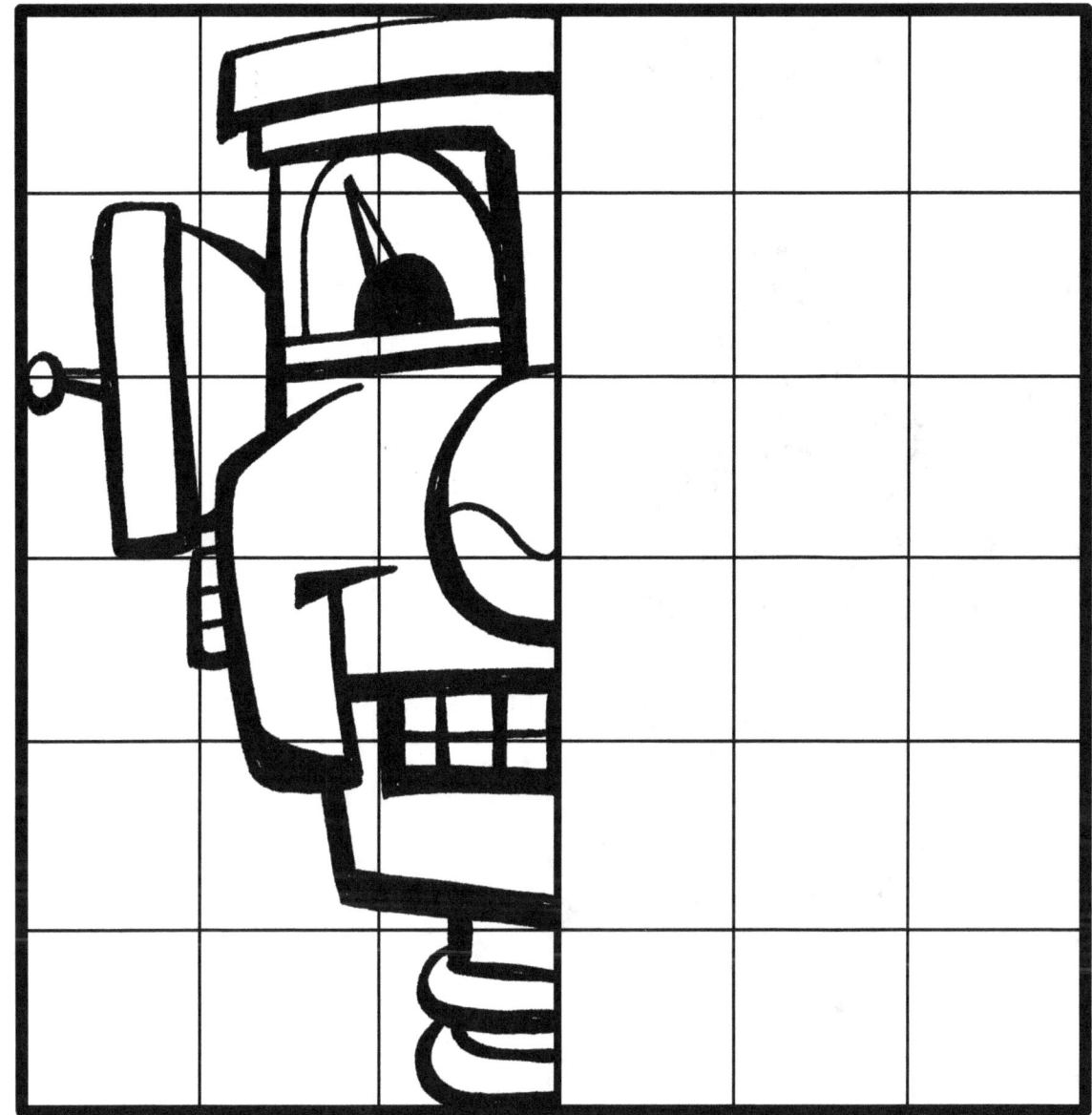

MR. JOBOTO

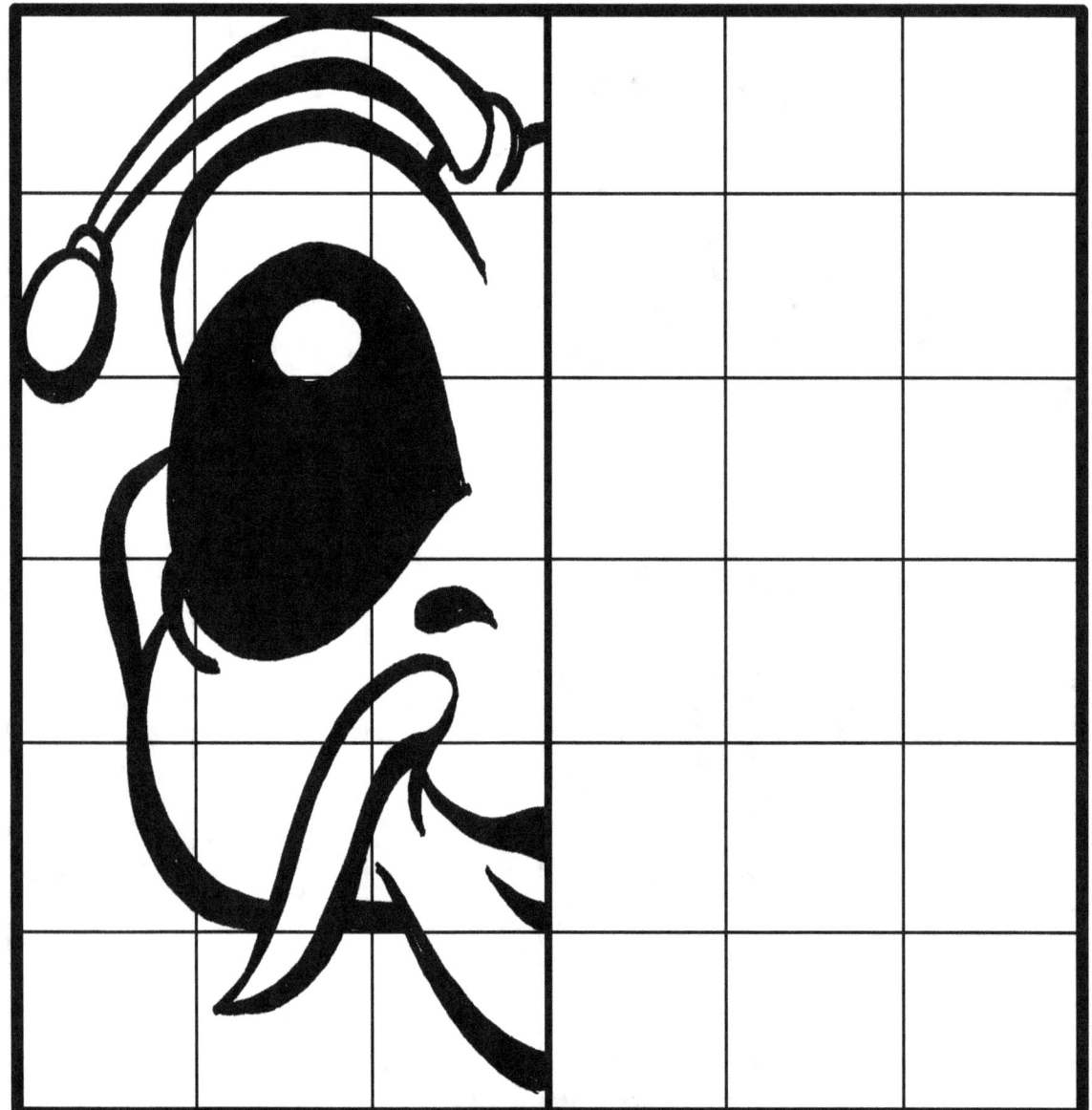

MANTENNA

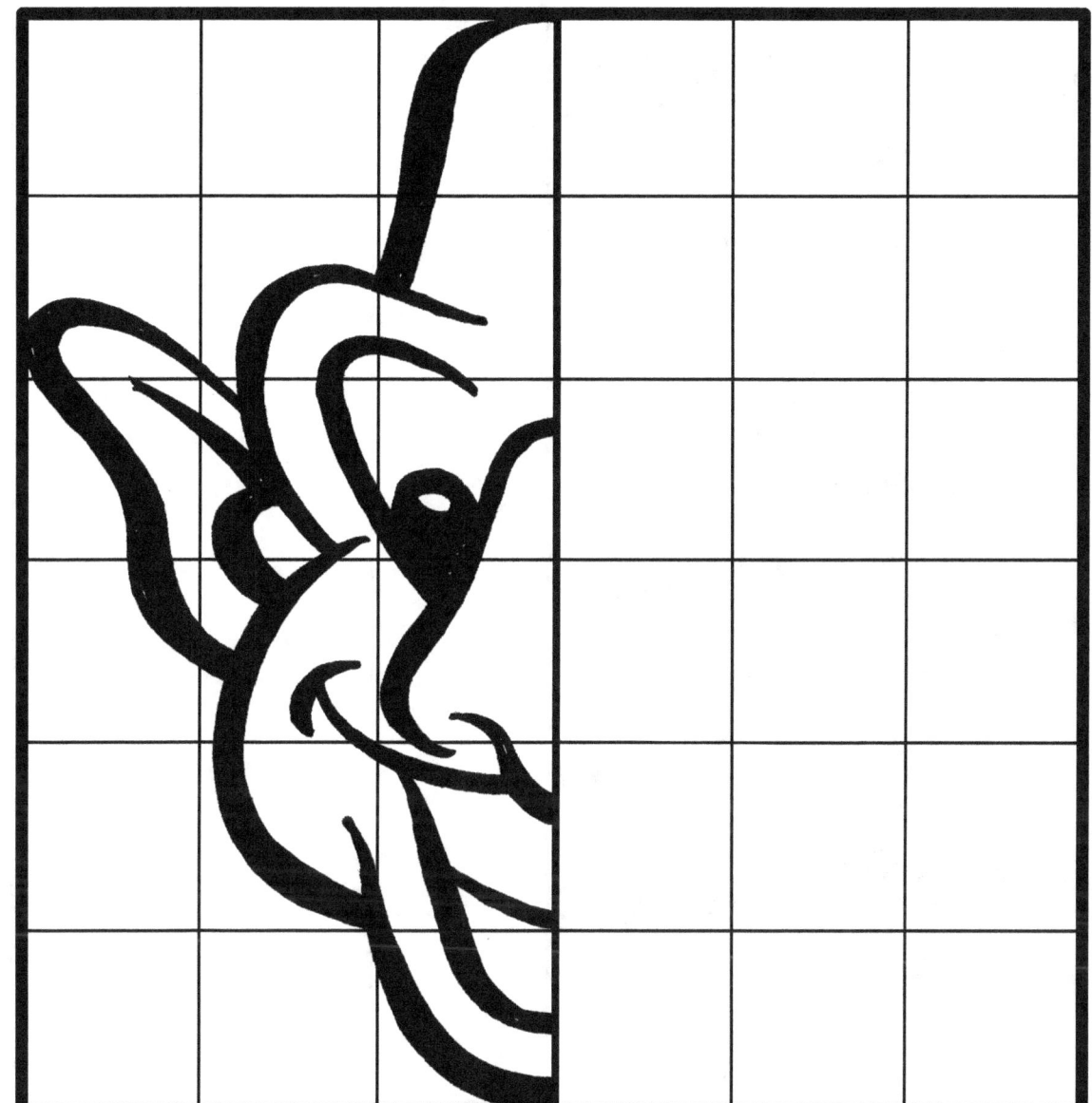

POINTDEXTER

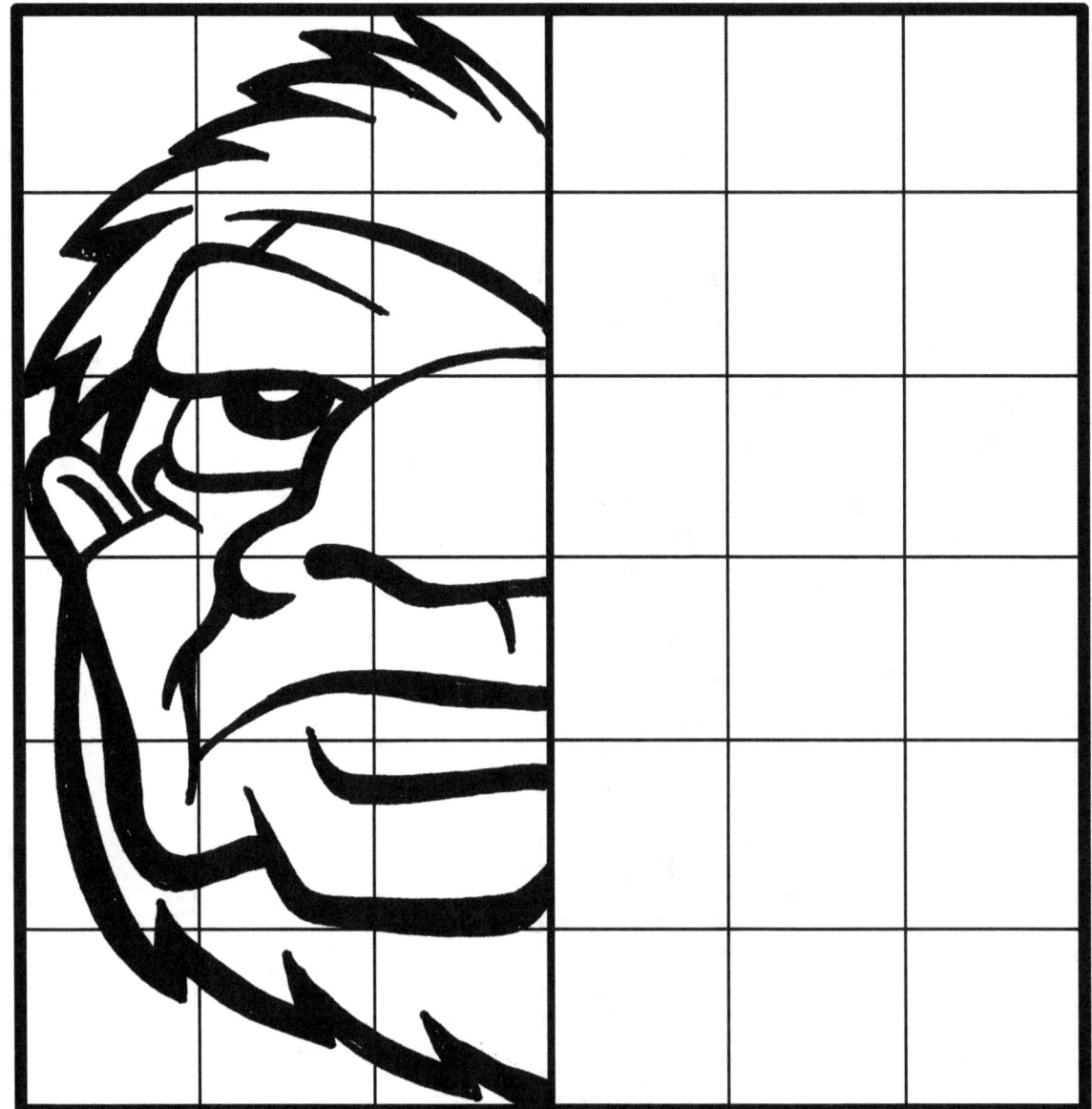

LEONDERTHAL

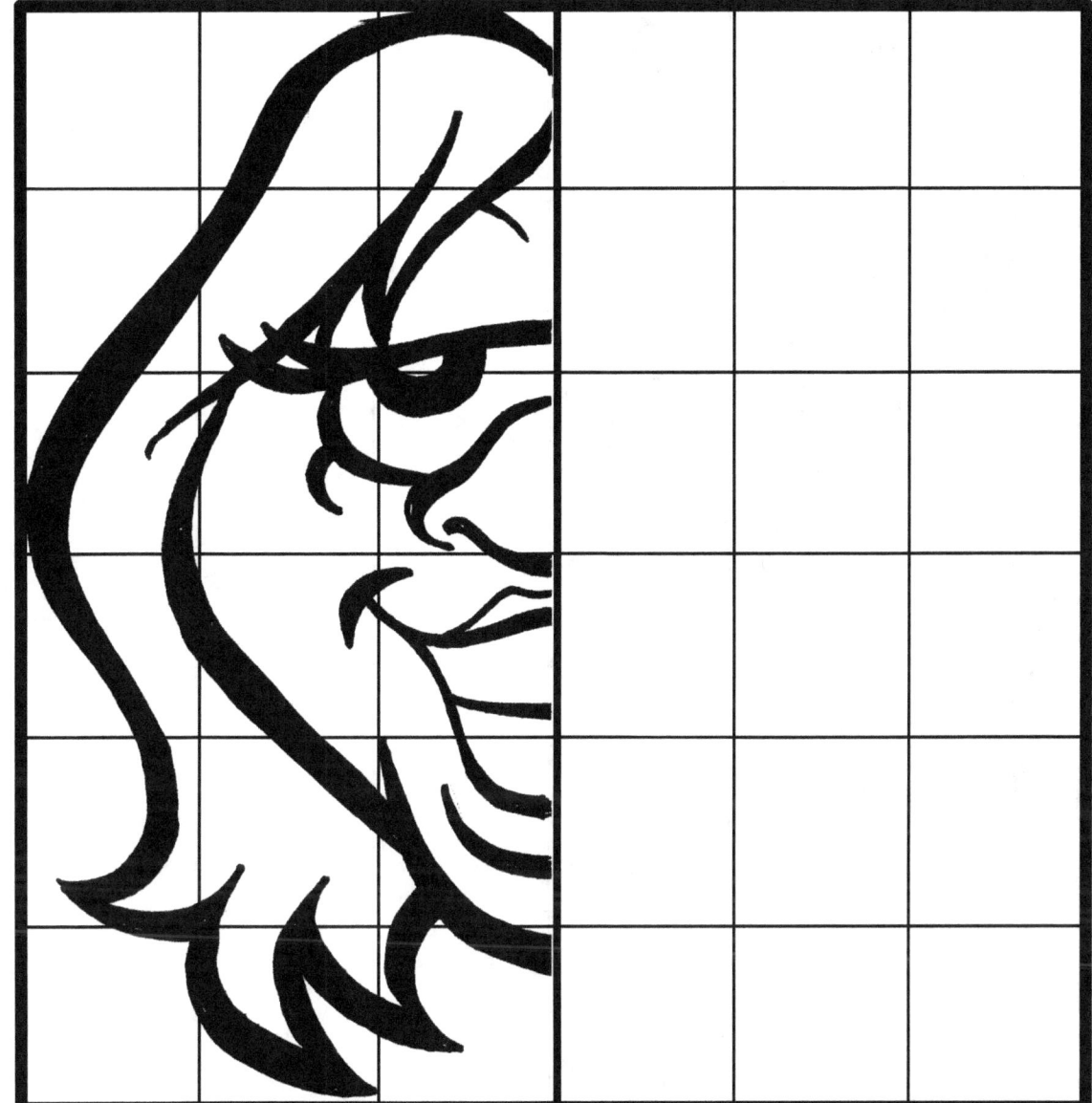

SHELLY

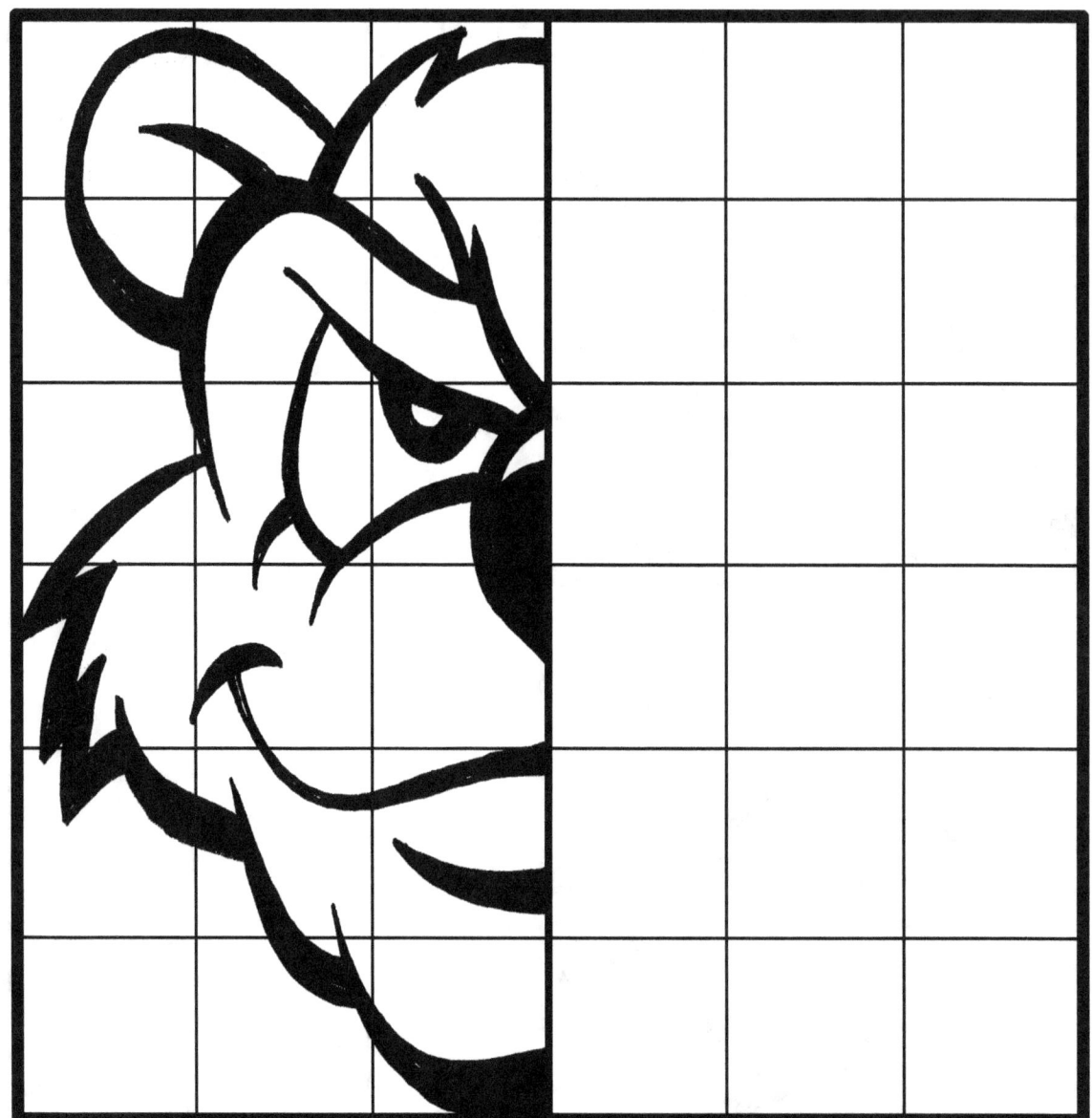

BRUINATOR

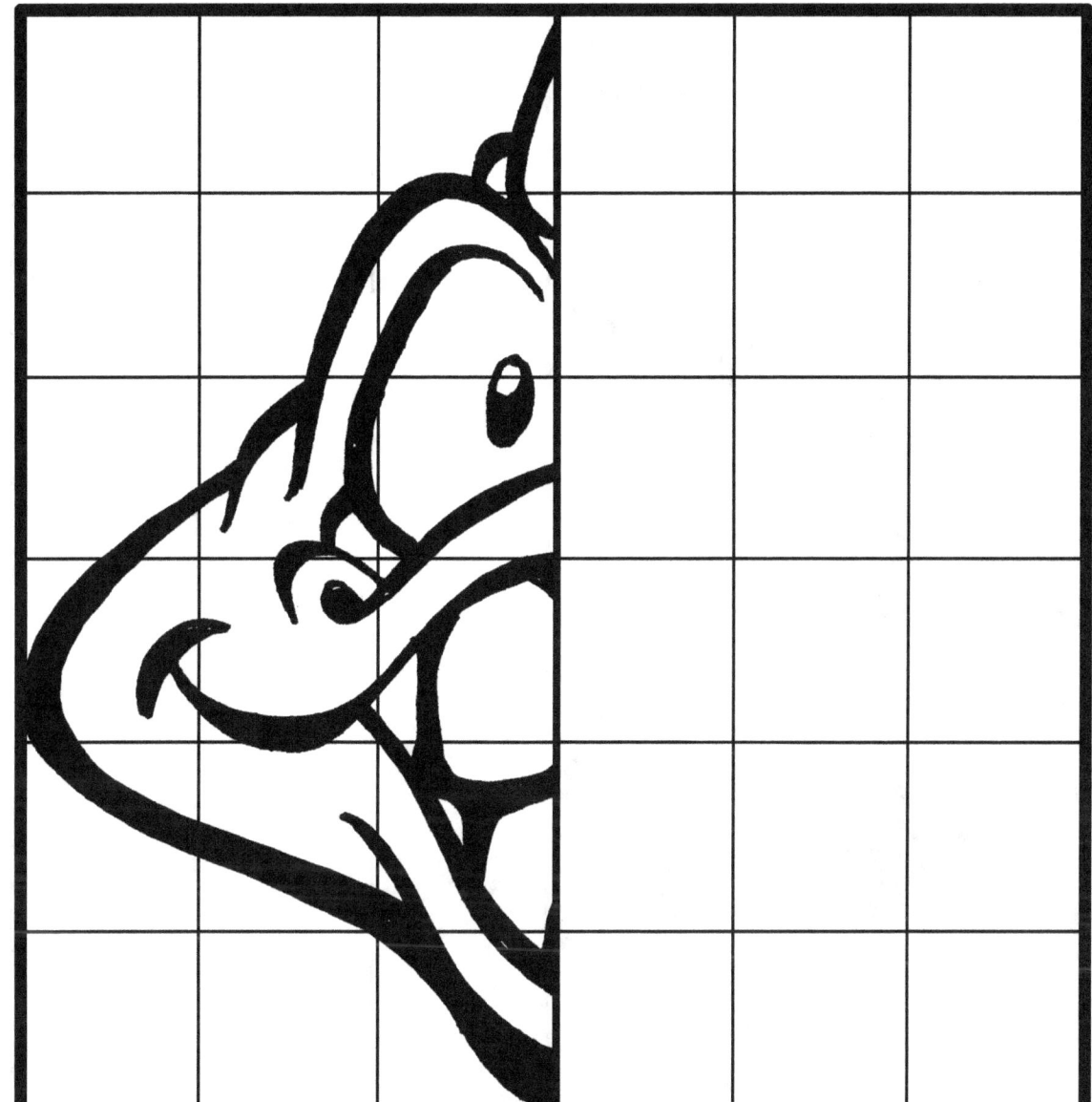

BLOMBO

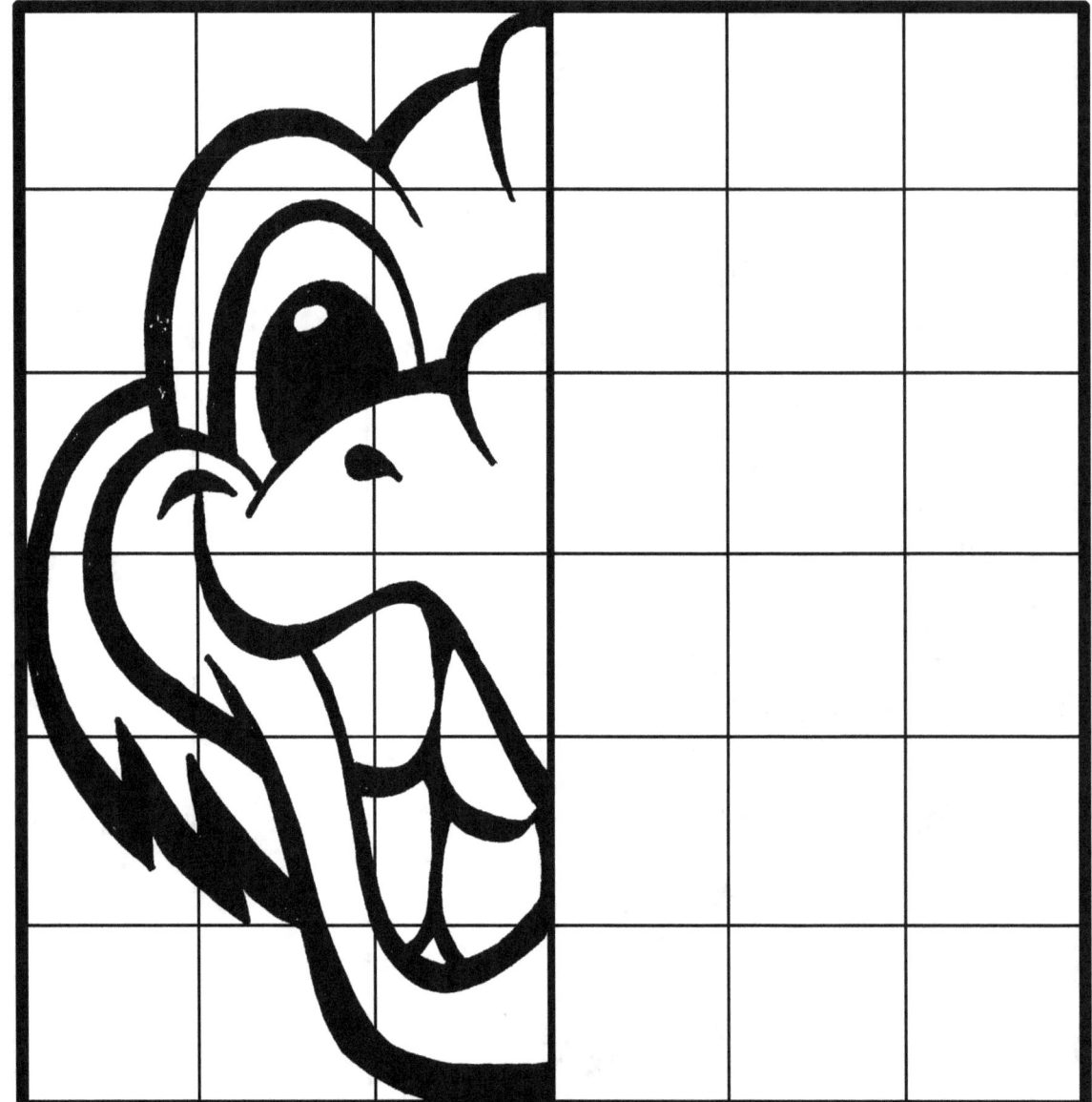

SQUONK

Now that you have finished a bunch of mine, finish me and then try a few of your own. On the next few pages are some blank grids. Draw half a face up to the middle line and then finish it just as you did all of mine. Have fun!

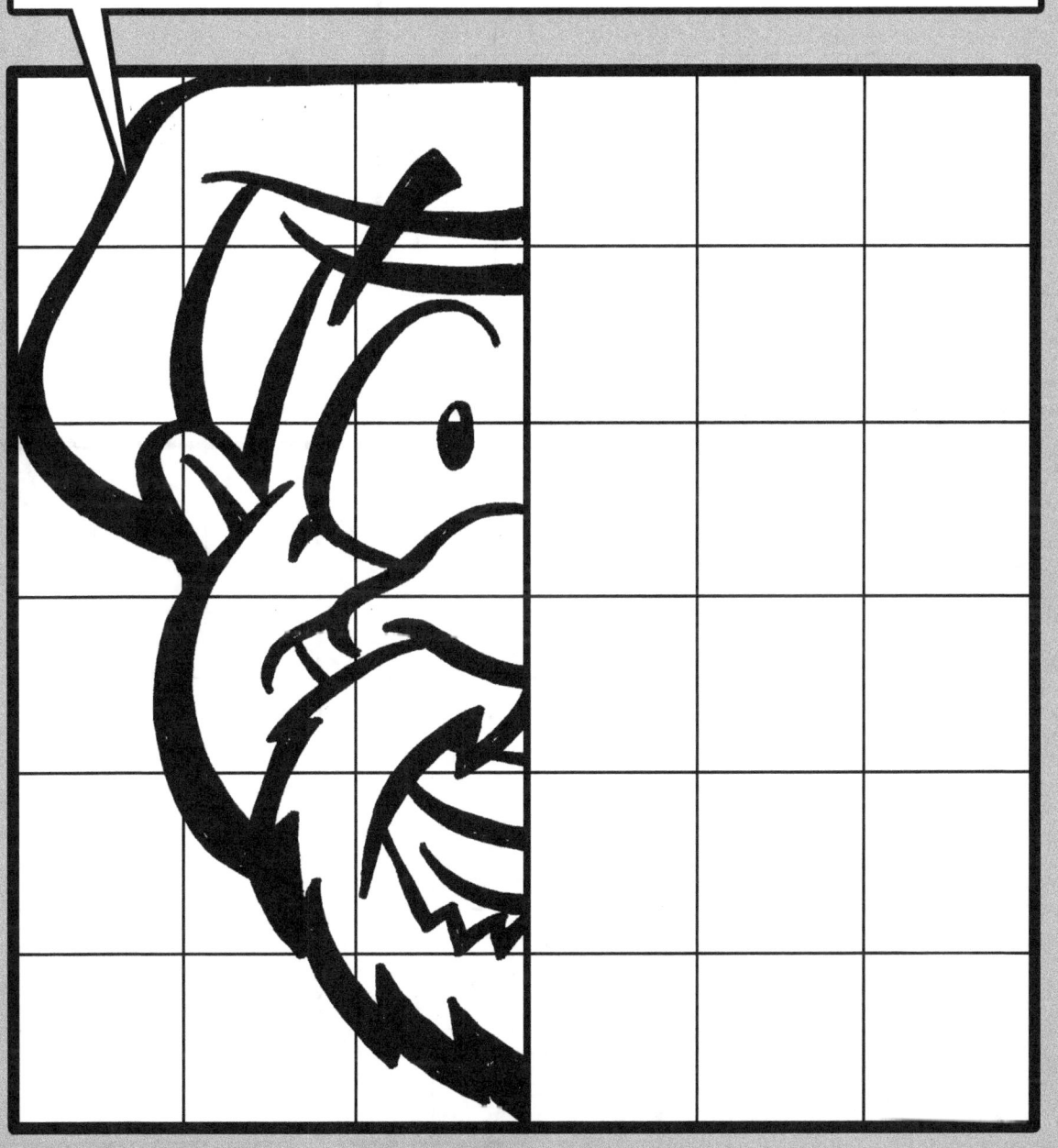

For more resources to build your creativity go to dweisscreative.com